LOOKING BACK

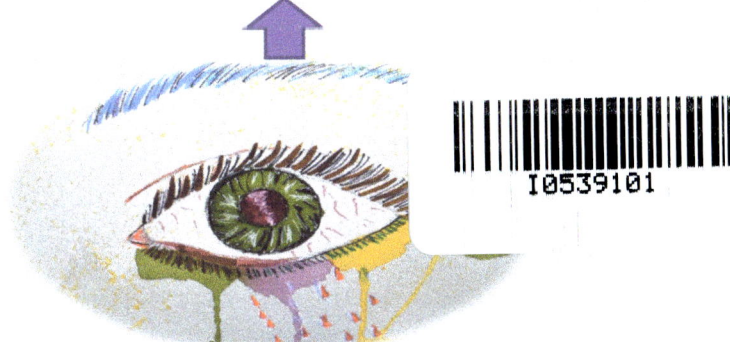

LOOKING FORWARD

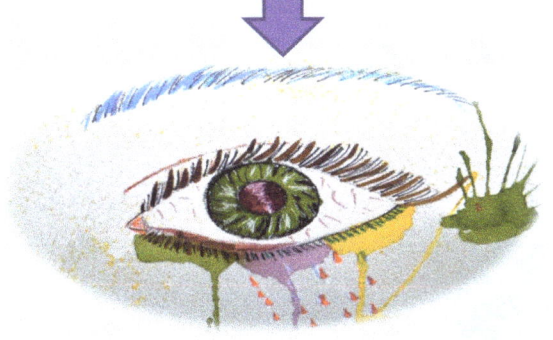

Poetry written by a father and husband dedicated to his
murdered son and his wife, a victim of Pancreatic Cancer

RALPH L MYERS

Printed in the United States of America

ISBN 979-8-89114-194-0 (sc)
ISBN 979-8-89114-195-7 (e)

Library of Congress Preassigned Control Number: 2025910901

2025.06.19

MainSpring Books
5901 W. Century Blvd
Suite 750
Los Angeles, CA, US, 90045

www.mainspringbooks.com

Tom A Myers	Francine J Apostolos-Myers
Born 12/29/67	Born 11/1/43
Murdered 7/24/93	Died from Pancreatic
	Cancer 9/15/15

After the murder of my son Tom in July 1993, I began writing these poems to (hopefully) cope with my grief of losing him healthily. The poems, although written about losing a loved one to violence, evoke similar feelings of grief and loss that are universal when someone loses a loved one, regardless of the reason or cause. Recently, I have had the privilege to read some of my poems at Hospice Grief Support meetings to those that were in attendance, and what I have done when writing this book of poetry is divide it into the various stages of grief one will go through when they lose someone dearly loved.

In September 2015, sorrow and grief again visited me when my wife of 49 years and love of my life Francine died because of the complications of Pancreatic Cancer and I want to rededicate this book of poetry to her as well as my son Tom and to all of those that have lost someone dearly loved and will forever be missed.

Ralph L. Myers June 30, 2016

About the Author

Ralph Myers was born in Indianapolis, IN on September 9, 1941 to Arthur and Leona Myers. Ralph has one brother, Phillip.

When asked, Ralph will quickly tell you that the three most important and happy events in his life are his marriage to Francine and the births of their son Tom and daughter Maria.

In 1968, Ralph,, his wife of less than two years, and their two-month-old son Tom moved from Indiana to California.

In 1970, on Christmas Day, Ralph and Francine were blessed by the birth of their daughter Maria.

Life for the Myers family was pretty every day until the fateful Saturday night of July 24, 1993. It was on this date that their son Tom, now 25 years old, was murdered while attending a party near his home.

Life and living as they had known it was turned upside down as Ralph, Francine and Maria were now cast into the class or status of survivors of a murdered loved one.

Since then and until retirement, Ralph has devoted his life to helping other victims of violent crime or their survivors. He has worked with California Senator Dianne Feinstein and Congressman Brad Sherman on behalf of a widow of a murdered husband. Ralph has also served as Chairperson of Congressman Sherman's Task Force on juvenile crime.

Because of the murder of his son Tom, Ralph has been active as a co-leader of a grief support group, "Parents of Murdered Children, Inc. Ralph has served on the advisory board of directors of "Justice for Homicide Victims," a victim's rights organization. He has also served on the advisory board of directors of the Nicole Parker Foundation, an organization founded by murder victim Nicole's mother, Lori Parker-Gladstein.

During his career in the Moving and Storage Industry, he owned a moving company. He was elected to and served as Chairman of the California Moving & Storage Association for one year.

Ralph has traveled to Washington, D.C., to lobby on behalf of a Victims' Rights Amendment to the U.S. Constitution introduced by Senator Feinstein and Senator Jon Kyl of Arizona. He also attended a conference there as Chairperson of Congressman Sherman's task force on youth violence.

Introduction

Saturday evening, July 24, 1993, my wife Francine and I realized a parent's worst nightmare, losing a child. On this evening, our son, at age 25, became a victim of murder.

Tom was single, still living at home with his mother and I, as well as his sister, who was away attending college in another part of the state. Tom was a good person who worked for me at my company. He was not involved in any gangs. His faithful love of life was surfing and snowboarding.

On that fateful, tragic evening in July, Tom came home from work at about 8:30PM and told his mom and me he was going to a going-away party for a friend who had joined the military. The party was less than 2 miles from our home in a part of the San Fernando Valley of Los Angeles that is considered relatively safe and where the crime rates are lower.

Tom left our home at about 9:30 PM to go to the party, stopping by an ATM to pick up some cash. He arrived at the party about 10PM. Around 10:30 PM, approximately six to eight carloads of teens, who police say were members of an Asian gang, accidentally found the party.

The party was a private party by invitation only, but this did not deter this group of gang members. They tried to crash into the party but were turned away. Instead of leaving as they were asked, they started a fight with some of the people who were invited to the party.

One of the party crashers went back to his car and retrieved a 9-millimeter handgun. This person fired it in the air, and then one of his buddies took the gun from him and started firing indiscriminately into the yard where the party was taking place. Our son Tom, we were told, was unaware of what was happening because he was inside the house. However, he walked out of the house and into the line of fire when the shooter started firing. Tom was hit twice in the chest and died moments after being shot. This happened thirty to forty-five minutes after Tom arrived at the party.

Fortunately, and miraculously, no one else was shot because the shooter got off eight shots in the direction of the crowd of partygoers. Two of those shots found their mark in our son Tom's heart and symbolically in the hearts of his mom, sister, grandparents, and many friends that night.

The person who murdered Tom was arrested, tried, and convicted of first-degree murder and is currently serving a 30-year-to-life sentence. He will be eligible for parole consideration in 2012. If my wife, daughter, or I are still living at that time we will do everything within our power to see that this person is not released back out onto the streets to claim another life possibly.

The poems I have written and included in this book continue to be my attempt to cope with my loss and a tribute to our son Tom.

Ralph L. Myers- Tom's Dad

Tom Myers surfing in summer of
1993. Shortly before he was
murdered.

Section I
Love and Loss

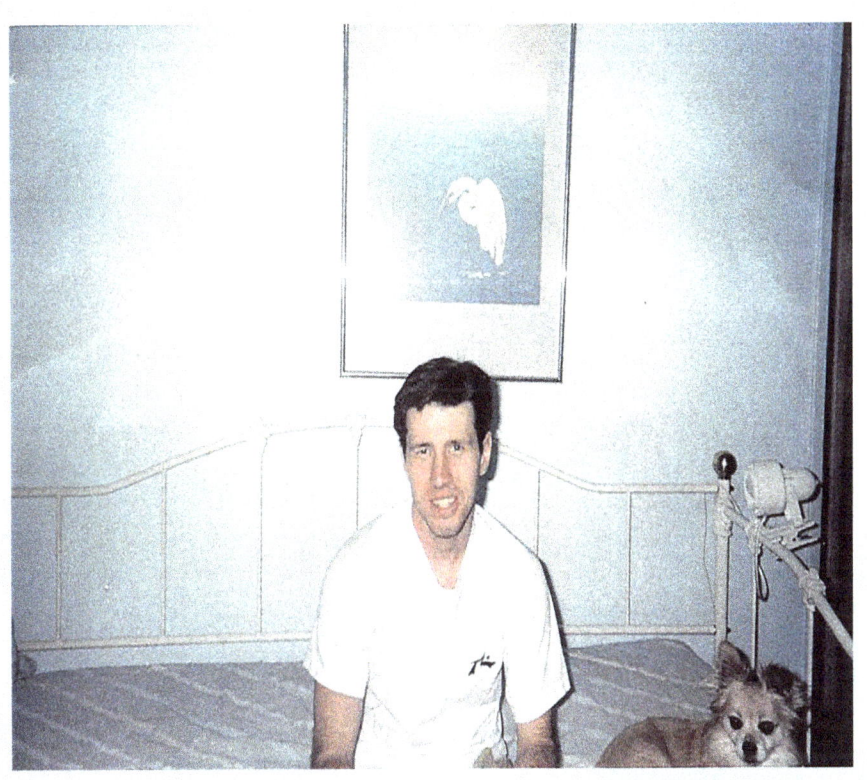

Tom and his dog are in his sister's room

1992

"A Dad's Love on Father's Day"

I wrote this poem on "Father's Day" in 1997 as a tribute to all dads everywhere who have lost a son or daughter to murder. That year, it had only been four years since my son Tom was murdered, and I was once more reflecting on the blessing from God and the privilege of being his father.

Ralph L. Myers

A Dad's Love on Father's Day

Loving precious child, it matters not if you were merely a baby, mischievous youth, handsome young man, or beautiful young woman when you were forever taken away from me, your protector, provider, counselor, and most importantly, your Dad, your friend.

My love for you, the moment I first saw and held you, my beautiful, tiny, helpless baby, cannot be measured. It is without limit, cannot be altered, and will never end.

Life has a way of passing us by so hastily. Why does it seem as though only yesterday I bounced you on my knee, gave you a new puppy, wiped away tears from your eyes, comforted and teased you, yet always reassured that I, your father, will always love you, and on me you can forever depend?

As days, months, and years go by, filled with memories of joy and happiness, sorrow and sadness, I spend another Father's Day thinking of you, my precious child, and thanking God for allowing me to be your Dad. Believing with all my heart that your spirit, your soul, is free from all sorrow, grief, and pain, in a place of serenity and beauty. Your memories are forever tucked away in my heart, guiding me onward and helping me overcome life's heartaches and disappointments. As I, your Dad, your Father, continue to go beyond the tragedy, enabling me to transcend.

Ralph L. Myers
Father's Day
June 15, 1997

"*Again, another July 24*"

As a parent of a murdered child can and will readily attest, each year on the date or anniversary of their child's murder, it is indeed a challenging day.

I wrote "Again another July 24" in 1997 on the third anniversary of my son Tom's murder while visiting his grave site.

The words I wrote are a conversation I had with him at his final resting place, letting him know that I would never forget him and that he would always be missed and loved by me and the rest of his family, particularly his mother and sister.

Ralph L. Myers

Again, another July 24

Again, the calendar reads yet another July 24.

Again, loved ones remember, and together they grieve on another July 24.

Again, and as always, I think of you, my son
Tom, on this, yet another July 24.

Again, a year has passed rapidly, yet it sometimes feels
agonizingly slow on this yet another July 24.

Again, on this yet another July 24, I visit your grave
instead of the warmth of our loving home.

Again, the pain of remembrance once more sears our
hearts, as we are reminded of the events that took place
four years ago on the night of yet another July 24.

Again, I am here, my son, at your final resting place, as I will always be on
future anniversary dates as each one of them becomes yet another July 24.

Ralph L. Myers
July 24, 1997

"Alone we survive"

I wrote this poem on May 3, 1996, just two months shy of the third anniversary of my son's murder. In this poem, I attempted to convey what I feel is a feeling of isolation a survivor of a murder victim feels as they continue to live and exist in a world that often seems oblivious, for whatever reasons, to their plight, which causes us to feel alone as we fight to survive our loss.

While this feeling may not entirely be true or the same for all survivors of murder victims, it sometimes, if a few times, feels we are in fact alone as we survive while being surrounded by other family members and friends.

Ralph L. Myers

Alone, We Survive

Every waking moment is interrupted only by the
peace and tranquility of sleep-induced hours.

Surrounded by the masses of humanity, oblivious to our not
chosen plight. The loss of our loved ones to violence gives cause and
reason for pessimism. As our outlook on justice and life sours.

Admonished by poet Milton, "No Man Is an Island,"
while we may be encouraged by family and friends,
we dwell within ourselves. Alone, we survive.

Praying for relief from our emotional suffering and pain. Constantly
searching, seeking logic and reason why the unspeakable happened on one
particular day? Why did sorrow come to pay us a visit, and sadness arrive?

Mother, father, sister, or brother, only yesterday were you alive.

Son, daughter, husband or wife, grandparent, or grandchild,
your lives were ended by murder. We are left alone with our
grief and emotions, innermost feelings. While existing in an
overcrowded world, we have been isolated. being given no other
options. Our mold has been cast and alone we survive.

Ralph L. Myers
May 3, 1996

"Forever your child"

I wrote and dedicated this poem to my son and daughter's mother and my wife on Mother's Day in 1994. This was less than one year since the murder of our son. It is a love poem from a mother's children, even if one of them is no longer living.

Just as the title states, "Forever your child," the same is true for the mother, as she will forever be your mother.

Ralph L. Myers

Forever Your Child

Mom, I was with you before the beginning of time. Before, Deity created the heavens and the earth, and the world evolved into being.

Preordained to be Mother and child, your love's depth is unlimited.

Our spirits together gave cause for the heavenly
bodies to glimmer and shine.

Together, we are the brilliance and fragrance of a budding rose.

A glistening sparkle of the drop of morning dew.

The vibrancy of colors comprises a sunrise and a sunset.

A glacial purity and stark beauty of the earth
being swathed in a new-fallen snow.

Or the crashing crescendo of pounding surf.

Mom, when you observe any of these, we are forever your children.

Dedicated to Tom and Maria Mom, Francine, by her loving
husband, Ralph, on Mother's Day, May 8, 1994

"In Remembrance we are here"

I wrote and read this poem at a rally for a "Week without violence" held in Pasadena, CA on October 15, 1995, for and in memory of all persons that have, are, or will suffer acts of violence committed against them during their lifetime. It was my appeal and message to society of the impact that violence has not only upon the victims but also on society as well.

Ralph L. Myers

In Remembrance We Are Here

In memory of our loved ones, who, because of violence,
are no longer here. In remembrance, we are here.

Our united voices speak out in their name and on their behalf because
they have been silenced forever. In remembrance, we are here.

Mothers, Fathers, sisters, and brothers deprived of their love
and seeing them grow are left with only memories. Each of us in
attendance and all of society robbed of their contributions and
potential greatness are something we will never know. Taken from
our presence, it is for them, in remembrance, we are here.

To the grandparents, other relatives, and countless friends, the loss
of our loved one has exacted a profound and immeasurable, painful
toll. For their grief and agony, in remembrance, we are here.

Crime and violence are without prejudice. With a bias towards none,
if allowed, it claims its victims all, regardless of race, creed, gender, or
color. Crime and violence have no boundaries, intent on sparing none,
yet eager to claim all. Realizing this, in remembrance, we are here.

For the abused and battered women and children suffering in silence,
existing in fear their pleas for help must be heard and not fall on deaf
ears. A victim of domestic violence there is one courtroom of justice
where your voices will be heard, the courtroom of public opinion where
equal justice will be served. For you, in remembrance we are here.

A week without violence, which to many is merely an admirable,
desired goal. To those of us who have already lost someone its meaning
has heartbreaking significance. To all of those not yet a victim, this
candlelight vigil represents hope and our prayer that no more of
you or your loved ones will ever be added to violence's ever-growing
roll. For this reason, as well as in remembrance, that we are here.

Ralph L. Myers
October 15, 1995

"July 25"

While July 24, 1993, will always be the worst day of my life, the next day is probably the second worst. I say this because it was early in the morning on July 25, 1993, that the homicide detectives came to the front door of our home to notify my wife and me that our son Tom had been murdered.

My wife was still sleeping soundly when I answered the door and was told that our son had been murdered the evening before. When I heard the doorbell ring, I thought it was some of my son's friends coming to pick him up to go surfing. I did not know or even suspect it would be members from the Los Angeles Police Department's Robbery-Homicide bureau coming to tell us such horrible and life-altering news.

I will never forget going into our bedroom and waking up his mother and telling her what I had just been told: our son, our Tom, was dead as a victim of murder.

Also, I will never forget her tears and screams of anguish as she held onto me, as together we went into our living room to talk to the two detectives.

Ralph L. Myers

July Twenty-Five

The sky is gray, and the stillness fills the morning air.
The year is nineteen ninety-three, July twenty-five.

A day, a year, like a clone of the one five years past. It seems
like only a heartbeat ago, yet it feels as though eons have passed
since the year nineteen ninety-three, July twenty-five.

Our heart was broken, our lives forever changed as two
messengers of sorrow and despair paid an unwelcome visit to
our home. Advising that Tom's life had been taken. No longer
was he alive on that early morning of July twenty-five.

Five years have passed, and only one thing remains the same. We continue
to exist in our grief and pain as we endure another July twenty-five.

Ralph L. Myers
July 25, 1998

"Rose Hills"

I wrote and read this poem at the annual crime victims' memorial service held at Rose Hills Cemetery in Whittier, CA, on April 18th, 1998. The memorial service was held during National Victims' Rights Week and was sponsored by Justice for Homicide Victims, one of the victim rights organizations in which I was active at that time.

Those in attendance at that memorial service were parents, grandparents, siblings, and friends of murder victims gathered in memory of their murdered loved ones.

The "JHV" organization has established and donated a "state of the art" touch screen computer memorial at this cemetery where a visitor can go and enter the name of a victim that is in the memorial's archives and hear an audio presentation by that victim's loved ones and see a pictorial history or perhaps even a video of the murder victim.

Ralph L. Myers

Rose Hills

Once again, our journey through life returns us to this chapel.
Overlooking the serene settings, lush green manicured acres
dotted with marble markers at the graves of loved ones are
remembered, at this memorial park called Rose Hills.

We are the survivors of those victims who were recently taken,
or perhaps years ago. Living reminders of loved ones lost. We are
examples of the plague of society and its inconceivable ills.

Continuing our fight.

Those victims are not forgotten or cast aside by a system that all too often
ignores the enormous burden placed upon them. We seek and simply
ask that we, too, shall have a measure of some Constitutional Rights.

Loving sons, precious daughters, fathers, mothers,
brothers, sisters, husbands, or wives,

Today, we honor the memories of your violently shortened lives.

Grandparents, grandchildren, relatives, or friends.

Every deserving victim of the brutal deeds of others, we gather here once
more in our annual tribute. Seeking the mercy and protection of a loving
God, we ask that our pain, like an overpowering thirst, be quenched.
That violence is reduced, becoming as nearly non-existent as He would
decree. We end this victim's memorial as another year of memories ends.

Ralph L. Myers, April 18, 1998

*Given at the Crime Victim's Memorial Service
during Victims' Rights Week*

"Six Days in July"

I wrote this poem as a record of the wide gamut of emotions experienced and the events that took place from July 24, 1993, to and including July 29, 1993, at the burial of our son.

Those "Six Days in July" are the worst days of our lives, and I think it is fitting that our emotions were preserved for anyone who may read this book of poetry and this poem. To me, I believe I have captured the devastation, heartbreak, and loss that is unique to a parent, sibling, relative, or friend of a murder victim.

Ralph L. Myers

Six Days in July

Days turn into weeks, weeks into months, and months into years.

Six days in July, forever molded and stamped in our memories,
bring back sorrow and fill our eyes with tears.

July 24, 1993

Our Tom's life was taken.

Loved ones and friends deprived people whose lives he touched,
and if given the choice, he would never have forsaken.

July 25, 1993

Homicide Detectives at our front door arrived.

Their sad, undesirable duty to advise.

Tom had been murdered; he was tragically no longer alive.

July 26, 1993

The arrival of this, another day, when time seemed to have ceased.
Placing our lives into a strange, disbelieving nothingness. While family
and friends continued to phone or arrive, displaying heartbreaking
sorrow, supporting each other as the realization and impact increased.

July 27, 1993

Unplanned funeral arrangements and obituaries prepared.

Discussions with the priest, continued outpouring of
sympathy and emotional pain, and efforts at uplifting our
sorrow-laden spirits. Our life journey continues as past
joys and present sorrows are intimately ensnared.

"July 28, 1993

A memorial service was held as the chapel was overflowing
with physical presence and heartfelt thoughts and memories of
Tom, which were so beautifully and tearfully expressed.

Eulogized and placed in perpetual memories, all in
attendance are embraced by Tom's love and by his young,
shortened life. Their saddened hearts are caressed.

July 29, 1993

Funeral Mass and service were beautifully and appropriately
held. Reflecting the events and love of Tom Myers' brief life
has concluded. As the hundreds in attendance accompany
Tom in a lengthy funeral procession to his final resting
place, that is peaceful and serene, yet not secluded.

After many family members and friends have since departed,
Tom's mother, Francine, and his father, Ralph, spend one
final moment alone with him in a tearful goodbye. We
love you, Tom, as we end these six days in July.

Ralph L. Myers
July 23, 1995

Artwork by Tom A. Myers

"Spiritual Communion, Son to Mother"

I wrote and dedicated this poem to the mother of the murder
victim, Christopher Brown, based upon an incident she had
while walking his dog in a park across the street from their home.
His mother, Donna Brown, felt her son was letting her know
he was okay and, in some way, communicating with her.

Many survivors of murder victims feel or have felt that their murdered
loved one does or has sent them a sign. I have never experienced any of
these feelings. However, the closest thing to an experience like this was
a dream I had recently, in which my murdered son was somehow with
our one-year-old granddaughter, and she took her first step with his
encouragement. The next day, our daughter and his sister called while
visiting a foreign country with her husband and our granddaughter and
told us she had just taken her very first steps. So, I guess there can be
some unexplainable coincidences or happenstances, and I feel happy for
those who experience something like what I have written in this poem.

Sadly, Donna Brown, Chris's mother, died
from cancer about four years ago.

Ralph L. Myers

Spiritual Communion—
Son to Mother

Inexplicable occurrences deemed by worldly intellects merely coincidental
are often greeted with theoretical disdain, pious contempt, and cynicism.

It cannot be dismissed as imagined or fervent desire and an
overwhelming feeling of neither presence nor superstitious mysticism.

When a son and all the love he must give is taken needlessly,
unmercifully, and without benefit of reason from his father and
mother, spiritual reuniting can gratefully exist when sadness and
sorrow seem to overpower their very being. The warmth and love
emanating from the departed son may manifest unexpectedly.

A simple walk in the park, finding trivia of symbolic
and treasured significance, causes a resurgent flood of
remembered thoughts and indelible memories.

Yes, Mom, I am forever at your side and constantly with you.
Tell Dad of my love and all is and will be forever well.

Dedicated to Donna and Dennis Brown in
memory of their loving son Christopher

Ralph L. Myers
October 26, 1994

"The Time is Seven Thirty"

Too often, dates or events may be interpreted as coincidental or even ironic. It was more a sense of irony that our son entered our lives at 7:30 AM when he was born and left us at approximately 7:30 AM the morning after he was murdered, because it was at that time the homicide detectives came to our door to tell us about his murder.

I have infused this poem with a sense of irony
as I reflect on our son's brief life.

Ralph L. Myers

"The Time is Seven Thirty"

The doctor came into the waiting room and told me we had
a new son. How proud I am to be a new father to our son
Tom this early morning. The Time is Seven Thirty.

It's Christmas morning, almost three years since Tom
was born. Hurriedly, the gifts are unwrapped as labor
pains begin. Our daughter Maria demands to be born,
to be let into our lives. The Time is Seven Thirty.

Where is the time going? Our son Tom is off on his first day of school,
eager to learn. Lunch box in hand, reluctantly, he kisses his mom goodbye
as she walks him to the school door. The Time is Seven Thirty.

Can it be possible that Tom is now grown, making his
way in a world of his own? Each morning, he leaves the
warmth of his home. The Time is Seven Thirty.

Soundly I sleep this July Sunday morn, awakened by a sound at
our front door. Two strangers were standing there. Their task
is to advise that our son Tom's life has been taken. His life cut
short; his existence is no more. Anguish and sorrow, overcoming
our souls. Trying to cope with this horror as it unfolds, I
glance at the clock, and it says The Time is Seven Thirty.

Ralph L. Myers
March 17, 1995

"Tom, you're thirty today."

Certain events in each of our lives are more significant than others. Our birthday is one prime example, as are certain other milestones we reach in our lives. One such milestone is turning thirty. My son was murdered at the age of 25, and five years later, he should have been with us to celebrate turning thirty, which is another significant birthday to be celebrated.

I wrote "Tom, you're thirty today," thinking about how we were forced to commemorate his 30th birthday instead of how we should have been able to.

Ralph L. Myers

"Tom, You're Thirty Today"

Tom, my son, you're 30 today.

Another year older, another birthday.

Big plans and a celebration should be in store for this milestone birthday.

Tom, your mom, and your sister visited you today.

As for me, your dad, I'll stop by too. But for how long, I really can't say.

Tom, it's so hard to feel any joy in what should
be a fun-filled day for you and us.

Tom, it's nearly impossible to believe it's been more
than four years since you were taken away.

Tom, you know you are loved, and we ask God to take care of you, while
you watch over us as we visit your grave on this another birthday.

Love Dad, December 29, 1997

By Ralph L. Myers, written in memory of Tom A. Myers.
Born 12/29/67 and murdered on July 24, 1993

"Yelling in Silence"

As I sit here in my office writing this and explaining the significance of each poem, in this poem, I am sitting in what was my son's room as he was growing up, and when he was murdered. To this day, nearly fifteen years later, we have partially preserved his room by displaying items that identify the things he loved and were special to him.

In May 1996, I wrote "Yelling in Silence" as I sat in this room, missing him and gazing upon some of the mementos that were a part of his identity.

Former California Attorney General Dan Lundgren used this poem in a speech he gave as he sought tough-on-crime and criminal legislation in California.

Ralph L. Myers

Yelling In Silence

Standing in what once was your home, your refuge, and
your room. I think, I gaze, and I grieve as the beating of
my heart pulsates in my brain, yelling in silence.

Surfboard, Snowboard, and a picture you once so carefully
drew stare back at me. Objects you loved, defining your youth, if
possible, would ask where you have gone and where you have been.
Merely stand alone in a corner of your room, yelling in silence.

I miss you, Tom; I love you, my son. What was done, what happened
to you, should not have. It should never have been. The sound of your
voice, your mischievous grin, are now only treasured memories locked
deep within my heart, my being, confined in my soul, yelling in silence.

Ralph L. Myers
May 28, 1996

"You are My Child"

This poem I wrote as a tribute to my son and in memory
of all the sons and daughters whose lives were so needlessly
and tragically cut short when they were murdered.

I have tried to capture the joy of what it means to be a parent and the gift
that has been bestowed upon them of a son or daughter. A gift, which,
as it turned out, was on loan to us as parents and had to be returned.

As you read this, especially if you are a parent or grandparent,
I am sure you will relate to the joys of having a child and the
responsibilities of being a parent as you guide your child through life.

I also feel that as a parent, you can also relate to what has been
referred to as a parent's worst nightmare of losing a child, no
matter what caused their death. But when the loss of a child is
due to murder, it is impossible to understand why such a horrible
thing happened. The only thing you are sure of is that the
murdered son or daughter was and always will be your child.

Ralph L. Myers

You Are My Child

Sounds of laughter, feelings of happiness, and expressions of joy are what we remember, treasure, and hold dear when our constant thoughts are on God's gift to us of our girl or boy.

You are my child.

Endowing you with values and traits of what's right, teaching and shielding you from wrong, and guiding your pathway through life on a journey that should have been long.

You are my child.

The absolute realization of horror, and the magnitude of sorrow, when you were so cruelly and callously whisked away by the evil and unthinkable deed of another, is so bad. It is magnanimously surpassed, overshadowed by the purest of truth and love. I was and always will be your dad, and you are my child.

Ralph L. Myers

June 4, 1995

Written in memory of my son Tom Myers and all the other sons and daughters whose lives were too brief.

"You came to us, Tom."

Less than a year after my son Tom's murder, and as I tried to sort
things out in my mind and grieve, I wrote this poem in tribute
to him. I attempted to express the love that a parent has for their
child and the utter feeling of sadness when you lose a child.

Losing a child to murder robs that son or daughter of ever being able to
fulfill a life of what should have been, as it does those that are left behind.

Ralph L. Myers

"You Came to Us, Tom"

One cold Indiana winter's morn, safe and protected in
your mother's womb—You came to us, Tom.

Clothed and secure in your parents' love

You came to us, Tom

Given to us through an act of love

You came to us, Tom

Our concern and love for you instill values and respect for
all. So that all other lives your life touched would feel the
warmth and compassion existing within your being

You came to us, Tom

Bursting with childhood energy and curiosity,
ever so mischievous, yet ever so innocent

You came to us, Tom

Progressing through childhood, young boyhood, into young
adulthood, life's challenges were strewn in your pathway. We were
always there for you, supporting, cajoling, and encouraging you

You came to us, Tom

Your life, like a beautiful flower, was plucked and is now part of a
magnificent bouquet. One whose beauty and now that you are a treasured
and loved memory to all of us who knew and loved you, your mother,
sister, loving Grandparents, relatives, and many friends, are thankful
to God that even if only for a little while, you came to us, Tom.

*Written and dedicated to our Loving son Thomas Arthur Myers
by his Dad, Ralph L. Myers, February 20, 1994*

"Big Bear."

One of Tom's loves was snowboarding. Since Big Bear is about two hours from Los Angeles, he and his friends frequently went to Big Bear Mountain to snowboard.

I wrote this poem while my wife and I were visiting Big Bear for a weekend. We stayed at the base of the mountain, right at the ski-lift area, and I could picture Tom and his friends snowboarding down the mountain.

If only the mountain could talk, revealing stories from its past, which now would include my son Tom.

Tom, I hope you have found a "Big Bear Mountain" in Heaven and are happy and carefree.

Ralph L. Myers

"Big Bear"

Big Bear, I stand in awe of your beauty, where the
mountain air is clean, crisp, and clear.

Reaching majestically towards heaven since the beginning of
time measured by man, century by century, year by year.

If only you could tell your myths and legends recorded on the
sound of the wind rustling through fragrant pine trees. Myths
and legends are handed down from generation to generation.

All were playing intricate parts of Big Bear Mountain,
a manifestation of the beauty of God's creation.

In a not-too-distant past, a young man named Tom was
here challenging your snow-whitened slope.

Snowboard in tow, happy and carefree, a life full
of promises of future successes and hope.

Tom was murdered and taken away by someone
evil, but it was not meant to be.

No longer can he challenge your majestic slopes, racing
against the unknown as he once did, blazing downhill.

Tom, in your memory, your mom, sister, and I are here, reminiscing
and marveling at the frozen beauty, nature's icicles of frozen tears
created by God and you, on this mighty mountain of Big Bear.

Ralph L. Myers
November 20, 2000

"Day of Joy, Day of Sorrow"

In August of 2002, while reading some of the posts made by mothers who have lost their child to murder and what that must feel like as a mother, I wrote the following poem. In this poem and from a man's viewpoint after reading comments made by several mothers, I wrote what the loss of a child or children to murder a woman may experience.

Men and women grieve differently, and what a woman might feel, mainly since she carried her murdered child in her womb, has to be entirely unique and probably impossible for a man to comprehend.

Ralph L. Myers

Day of Joy, Day of Sorrow

God granted you to her on this day of birth, a day of joy.

Loving child, girl or boy.

Created by an act of love.

God and his chorus of angels above celebrated your birth on high.

As you were placed in the protective arms of your mother.

Mortal though she is, she comforts your life and
protects you as only she can, unlike any other.

She was blessed with you to share the day of your birth,
the day of her joy, followed by countless other days.

All violently stolen, when you were taken from her and
this earth, cast upon all a horrible, sad day of sorrow. A
day, a loss like no other, can anyone compare?

Dedicated to all the mothers who have lost their child to murder.

Ralph L. Myers
August 2, 2000

"Forever"

On Memorial Day 1999, I read this poem I wrote for the Justice for Homicide Victims Memorial dedication at Rose Hill Cemetery in Whittier, CA. Also, I read this poem at the victims' memorial service conducted at Rose Hills in 2000, 2001, 2002, and 2003.

Ralph L. Myers

Forever

God hear us now as we offer up our prayers for
those that we loved who were stolen away.

When sorrow and grief knocked on our doors,
violently taking our precious ones—Forever.

It was not of their choosing to leave those who love
them behind, in sorrow and pain—Forever.

Victims deprived of their lives, dignity, and rights. We, as your
survivors, cry out. Giving sound to your silent voices, delivering
messages that will finally be heard. No longer will they fall
on deaf ears or seemingly uncaring hearts. We refuse to allow
them to be ignored as we speak for them now and forever.

We continue our labor of love. Drifting about on oceans of tears. Though
they are gone, we, the survivors, no longer here, gather together on this
Memorial Day. Dedicated in their honor, to all that have or will be lost
to violence and crime. This tribute, this memorial, promises each victim
will never be forgotten. The memory of their lives being recorded, etched
on the consciences of future generations. Will the pain experienced
by loved ones who are left behind be placed in perpetuity—Forever?

Ralph L. Myers
April 14, 1999

"Missouri Farm"

I wrote and dedicated this poem in memory of a Parent
of Murdered Children Topic Forum's son, Scott. Scott's
father, Philip, is an accomplished poet himself and has
posted many beautiful and poignant poems dealing with
life, particularly after the loss of a loved one to murder.

Philip lost his son Craig to murder, and then just a short time later, his
other son, Scott, who was very close to his brother, committed suicide.

Philip told of one of the last times he was with his son Scott on a farm
in Missouri, where they lived. He then again related about the time
he was at the farm after Scott's death, and memories of that last time
when he and Scott were there together came rushing back to him.

To lose one son to murder is more than can be dealt with by many victim
survivors but to lose a second to suicide is beyond all comprehension and
as far as I am concerned the murder of his son Craig has caused another
murder albeit suicide which is also referred to as "self-murder" by many
of the members of Parents of Murdered Children a grief support group.

Ralph L. Myers

"Missouri Farm"

As I drove my neighbor's big John Deere tractor the other day.

I took in the beauty of Mother Nature's palette of October's
Fall colors and autumn winds, cool, crisp, and clear, as God's
creatures cavorted about, their beauty a magnificent display.

A Red-Tailed Hawk perched on a fence post nearby.

Casts a cautious glance my way with a wary eye.

As if, and surely it was Deity's plan, the hawk led me
to a part of the fence that had been repaired.

Patched by my son Scott and me just last year, a time
for father and son to share a precious moment, a special
bond which, like no other, can be compared.

From upon high in an old oak tree the Red-Tailed Hawk watched
down as I brought John Deere to a pause. Watching as I once more
remembered my time with Scott, examining the repair we made,
helping our farmer friend not because he asked, we did it just because.

Immersed in thought, I suddenly heard Scott's voice as he clearly spoke,
"Dad hand me the hammer" I promptly obliged saying "OK here it is son".

Without thinking or doubting it wasn't Scott's voice even though he
was no longer with me on this Missouri farm. I smiled as I remembered
our time just a year ago, we laughed, we toiled together as only we
could as father and son. His voice I again heard its sound I had not
forgotten and once again we were together, our spirits reunited as one.

Ralph L. Myers
Dedicated to Philip in memory of his son Scott
October 15, 2000

"A Missouri Farm Road"
Charcoal Drawing by Ralph L. Myers
September 2005

"Scottsdale 2000"

On August 10-13, 2000, the National Organization of Parents of Murdered Children held their annual convention in Scottsdale, AZ. This convention is a time when members of the grief support group from all over the country get together in memory of their murdered loved ones.

Generally, when a business or trade organization has an annual convention, it is a fun time. The feeling I have tried to convey in this poem is the stark contrast between a business or trade association convention and that of thousands of survivors of murder victims.

Ralph L. Myers

Scottsdale 2000

Searing heat, another day of Augusts' Scottsdale Arizona's blazing sun.

Throngs of tourists descending on a city offering vacation relaxation and fun.

Convention site, for many businesses and causes celebre.

Has yet to host, yet to see such a gathering of society's product of violence. We as the survivors of homicide victims, Parents of Murdered Children, family, and friends who have suffered a loss which cannot be dismissed and is beyond description, beyond compare.

Our message from Scottsdale this conference week. World, hear our cries, listen to our pleas for it is not we the living but rather in remembrance of our murdered loved ones' silenced voices for whom we speak.

Ralph L. Myers

Dedicated to the 2000 Annual Parents of Murdered Children,
Inc. Conference held in Scottsdale, Arizona August 10-13, 2000

"Stolen Away"

In today's world, it seems murder and violence are the rule rather than the exception, and when you have had a loved one stolen away by murder, whenever we read the newspaper or watch television news, it again reminds us of our loss.

"In 'Stolen Away, ' I have tried to, even if only in some small way, explain to society the wide range of emotions, disappointments, and sorrow survivors of murder victims feel and experience, and how their lives have been forever changed.

Ralph L. Myers

"Stolen Away"

This morning's newspaper, radio, and TV news once more told
of someone's murder, of another killer the police now pursue.

Again, questions about why it happened are asked, and
reasons and excuses are routinely offered to explain.

Yet what is usually forgotten or ignored is the
murder victim's and survivor's pain.

A victim of circumstances, wrong place, wrong time, accepted as a fact.

But the victim was asleep in their home, working on
the job, when a brutal act ended their life.

Heartbreaking sorrow on that fateful day arrived by
a call on the phone or a knock on the door.

As they're told of a loved one's murder, the
survivors' lives have been changed forever.

How this could have happened, why it happened, might
never be known, and the loss can never be changed.

The celebration of life by a loved one's murder ceases to
be, and an unplanned funeral must be arranged.

Days, weeks, and years go by as survivors grieve, trying to cope.

Speaking out as the voice of their silenced loved one,
seeking justice in their name, with a fervent hope.

Confronted by those who care more for the rights
of the murderer cannot be understood.

Get on with your lives, you are told, wallowing
in grief and sorrow does you no good.

There, my friend, my story is told, of a survivor's plight.

When my world forever changed on that fateful night.

Please listen to the survivor's message now, not another day.

When someone dearly loved was murdered, stolen away.

Precious daughter or son, you were murdered and stolen away!

Husband, wife, brother, or sister, why did your
murder happen? I ask each passing day.

Mother, father, grandparents, or cousin, your
life should not have ended that way.

Special companion and friend, your memory
shines like a heavenly sent sunray.

Our message must be heard, you did not choose to
leave. You were murdered and stolen away!

Ralph L. Myers
November 11, 2000

Tom Myers, 1992 or 93

"We Held Hands"

I wrote this poem as a love poem to my wife and the mother of our murdered son. When I wrote, we had been married for over thirty years. As I am putting this book of poems together in this revised "Looking Back-Looking Forward, it is July 2016, and Francine died from Pancreatic Cancer in September 2015, and I finished this poem after her death, and the one now shown is the completed one.

"We Held Hands" is a chronological record of our journey and lives together as husband and wife, mother, and father, and now I am happy to say grandparents.

We all know the vows we take when we are married: We are there for each other, in sickness and health, in joys and sorrow, till death do us part." In the forty-nine years we have been married, I can say without hesitation that we have indeed experienced those conditions as stated in our marriage vows.

It has been tough at times, but through it all, "we have held hands" and never stopped loving each other. Without the love and support of my wife, Francine, Tom's mother, I do not think I would or could have survived the ordeal of his murder.

Ralph L. Myers

We Held Hands

Francine,

That night, nearly 50 years ago, I took you on
our first date. We Held Hands.

On that beautiful sunny day in June, as we stood before the
priest exchanging our wedding vows, We Held Hands.

On that cold December morn, you gave me life's greatest
gift of love when Tom was born, and We Held Hands.

Again, in December on Christmas morn, just three short
years had passed. You presented me with our Maria, the most
beautiful present I could get, and We Held Hands.

Many years and loved ones have passed our lives like
others filled with joys and sorrows, overcoming life's
many challenges, and as always, We Held Hands.

On that fateful day in July 1993 when our Tom was stolen away our hearts were filled with heartbreak and pain as we are once more in the presence of a priest laying Tom to his final rest, together we stood with tear-filled eyes, saying a final goodbye to our only son, and as always, We Held Hands.

In June 2012, we argued our case before the California Board of Parole that Tom's murderer should not be granted parole, set free to possibly victimize yet another family, inflicting the kind of pain, anguish, and sorrow we have been forced to endure. We Held Hands.

Just two short months later, you were diagnosed with Pancreatic Cancer and told the prognosis was dire. Together in the doctor's office as we received this news, We Held Hands.

Loving life, our daughter, son-in-law, granddaughter Atessa, grandson Keyvan, and I, you fought a valiant three-year fight defying the odds of letting the cancer win, going through debilitating chemo treatments. I was always by your side, and as always, We Held Hands.

I was with you at your side when your body could no longer continue to fight. I told you I would love you forever and asked God to embrace you as you entered the portal to eternity, softly kissing you goodbye, and as always, of course, We Held Hands.

Written by your husband, Ralph, this poem is a tribute to my wife, Francine, which I wrote during the 49 years we were together and married.

"A Day of Darkness and a Dawning of Light"

I wrote this poem on Easter Sunday, 2001, just four months before the September 11 Terrorist attacks. Of course, no one knew or even dreamed such a day of darkness could or would happen, just as those of us who have lost a loved one to murder would ever expect in their worst nightmares someone would murder their son, daughter, husband, wife, grandparent, or friend.

When a horrific event like this happens at that moment or on a day of darkness, we must hope and pray for a dawning of light. The Christian belief in Christ, his crucifixion, and resurrection exemplify a day of darkness and a dawning of light, as any story ever told, regardless of your religion or faith. There is and can be a new day and a dawning of light.

Ralph L. Myers

"A Day of Darkness— and a Dawning of Light"

On this Easter morning, we awakened to a
new day of promise, hope, and light.

I find a parallel between the story of Easter and our
lives of struggle and tragic plight as survivors.

As it was written in the Gospels of Matthew, Mark,
Luke, and John, when Jesus was crucified.

From the sixth hour to the ninth, darkness descended
upon all the earth until He gave up the ghost and
departed from His mortal life when He died.

Can be compared to the darkness that fell over our lives
when our loved one's life by murder came to an end.

Like the Temple's veil, our hearts were ripped open,
shattered, and broken. However, could we continue to
cope with these tragedies, survive, and transcend?

Now with the dawning of Easter morning filled
with promise, hope and redeeming light.

As the story of Easter in the Bible was told, He has arisen,
giving us all hope like this Forum, allowing us yet another
day to rejoice in the memories of our loved ones violently
taken away and, in their names, continue our fight.

Ralph L. Myers
Easter Morning, April 15, 2001

"The Forum of Hope"

Throughout this first section of "Love and Loss," I have often referred to the organization of Parents of Murdered Children and its "Forum of Hope." Those of us who have lost someone to murder can go on the internet at any time of the day and post whatever our feelings happen to be at that given moment.

Believe me, as a survivor of a murder victim, and depending on how recent and sometimes months or years later, after you have lost your loved one, it is a Godsend to have this outlet. I think it is also a lifesaver, as many survivors become so depressed and see no hope, and may feel "what's the use" and consider taking their own life.

On New Year's Eve, 2000, I wrote and dedicated this poem to my good friend Sue Veldkamp, a web designer who put this Forum of Hope on the. (Parents of Murdered Children) web page. POMC Sue has since died from the same illness as my wife, Pancreatic Cancer

If you want to see the rawest of emotions and feelings of a survivor of a murder victim, I encourage you to go to the web page POMC.com and click on the Forum of Hope link.

As the reader of this book of poetry, hopefully, you have not and will never lose someone to murder, but I think you will quickly understand what these survivors who have posted their innermost feelings have and are continuing to go through. One final and important thing is to read the comments, try to understand their expression, and not judge them.

Ralph L. Myers

The Forum of Hope

A Poem by Ralph L. Myers

We have suffered incalculable sorrow, heartbreak, and despair.

Losses of loved ones to a society possessed by hatred, violence,
and injustice is the common bond that we share.

Lives forever altered, emotional and physical well-being
unreasonably, tragically, in less than a heartbeat changed.

Day after day, month upon month, soon becoming year
after year, from family and friends through no fault
of our own, we have often become estranged.

Just as it seemed our lives we have lost, no
longer can we or do we want to cope.

For many, life and living have reached what feels like a
dark and everlasting bottomless pit. However, this "Forum
of Hope" offers a new gift of love and survival.

Now with the dawn of each new day, no matter
what sorrow, anger, or despair I feel.

I have a place to go to express my rage, vent my sorrow, and shed my
tears with others who will understand this, "Our Forum of Hope."

It gives us all a chance to perhaps recover, to get through darker
moments, and just "maybe" to be able to emotionally heal.

Ralph L. Myers

December 31, 2000

*Dedicated to Sue Veldkamp and all the survivors of
murder victims. We thank her for our "Forum of Hope"
and all my lifelines and other Forum of Hope members.*

Sadly, Sue Veldkamp died from Pancreatic Cancer in 2020.

"San Aleo Beach"

As I have mentioned several times, my son Tom loved to surf. One of my most significant memories of him and his surfer friends was when he was about 13 or 14 years old. I took Tom and three of his best friends to a beach near San Diego called San Alejo Beach. Surfers in Southern California note that it is an excellent surfing beach.

Many years later, after Tom's murder, my travels took me once more to the small town of San Alejo, and this time for the funeral of a business friend of mine.

I arrived at San Alejo early and had time to go to the beach again before the funeral services. Sitting in my car as I watched the waves break on the shore, I wrote this poem as I recalled that wonderful weekend I was blessed to spend with Tom and his friends.

Ralph L. Myers

San Alejo Beach

Azure colored ocean, blue cloudless sky.

Gentle breeze, white capped breaking waves peaking four feet high.

It was not so very long ago, in a not-too-distant past.

I brought you here, a happy time, surfing with your friends, catching
the next wave, carefree and sure your life and youth would forever last.

I stopped by this beach again today, Tom, thinking you should
be here instead of where you are. Thoughts that seemed
to make the breaking surf sound like a gentle sigh.

The seagulls cried mournfully for you.

Unfortunately, Tom, it was not meant to be.

So here I sit, writing this poem, praying to God that, like this
beautiful seaside creation of His, you have found as tranquil a
setting as possible, and your soul is happy and carefree.

I love and miss you.

Dad

Ralph L. Myers
May 26, 2000

Section II
Despair and Denial

Ralph L. Myers

Below are some of the usual remarks or comments
made as one attempts to grasp what has happened
when a loved one or acquaintance is murdered.

"This is a safe neighborhood!"

"Something like this never happens here!"

"I feel at such a loss, I don't know how I can cope with this!"

"Why am I being punished?"

"How could God allow such a horrible thing
to happen to me and my family?"

"Crime and Murder only happen in the seedy parts of town!"

"Broken Hearts-Shattered Dreams, the Legacy of a Crime Victim Survivor"

In writing this poem during March 1996, I was trying to put into a word picture the sadness and despair that the family and friends of a murdered loved one are left to deal with and cope with.

As the title of this book states, "Looking Back—Looking Forward," this poem encompasses all those feelings of the murdered loved one's life before they were killed, as those left behind look back.

This poem also looks forward to what might or should have been had the loved ones not been murdered.

Ralph L. Myers

Broken Hearts—Shattered Dreams—The legacy of a Crime Victim Survivor

Broken are the hearts and shattered are the dreams of the mother,
father, grandparent, relative, friend, sister, or brother.

Through murder and abuse, the taking of our loved ones'
lives has caused sorrow, grief, and pain. The depths of which
are immeasurable and incomparable to any other.

Our hearts have been broken, and our dreams have been shattered
when on that horrible day, anguish came to our door.

Taking away all our loved ones' tomorrows, their loving presence gone.
Leaving us only treasured memories, nothing else, nothing more.

What was to have been the legacy of a life?

Bestowing upon us all blessings of a future with children, grandchildren,
and loving support as father, mother, son or daughter, husband, or wife.

Instead, terrible, cruel, unforgivable acts of violence inflicted upon
them have bequeathed a lifetime legacy of sorrow and sadness.

Leaving behind survivors, victims of crime, with broken hearts
and shattered dreams. Where once there was a person whose life
was full of joy, happiness, and enthusiasm, with the hope that all
their tomorrows would be filled with promise and gladness.

Ralph L. Myers
March 30, 1996

"Impossible, not in My Neighborhood"

The feelings I have described in this poem are the
epitome of society's denial that terrible things can and
do happen in so-called "safe neighborhoods."

I have to admit that as a parent living in what is perceived to be a safe
and relatively crime-free neighborhood, I was one of those who shook
my head when I read a newspaper account of a violent crime being
committed. Or I would change the channel on the television when a news
report of a murder came on. I did so primarily because (I thought) those
things always happen in a bad part of town and for anything to happen
like that where I live is simply "Impossible, not in my neighborhood."

On the night of July 24, 1993, just how wrong I was
brutally and forcefully brought home to my family
and me when our son was murdered.

Ralph L. Myers

"Impossible—not in my Neighborhood"

The morning sunlight casts a shimmering brilliance on a shroud of this day's early dew. With the dawning of another day, I have been granted a reprieve from yesterday's setbacks and disappointments. Given more hope and promise as today begins anew.

A cup of coffee and the daily newspaper in hand. Another night of senseless violence and wanton criminal deeds is revealed.

My senses of outrage, sadness, and empathy for the victims are lessened, nearly deadened by the distance between where I live and where the horrific acts were committed, many by juveniles whose criminal records have been sealed.

Thank God if those things must happen, their occurrence is elsewhere and surely could not occur in my safe neighborhood.

The reward of my hard work and effort has manifested, allowing me to live in a community where crime is nearly non-existent. I feel secure in the knowledge that my children and their friends are decent and good.

Days, weeks, and months swiftly become years. Time passes
by as the enigma of violent crime continues to escalate.

The reasons for and the causes why are perpetually in debate.

Our neighborhood is still perceived to be safe. It seems
to be an island surrounded by gangs and crime.

Urgent action must be taken while there is still time.

New victims are added to the statistics as those figures grow.

Yet another mother weeps when her son or daughter is added to the toll.

Once more, as countless times before, we bid
farewell to our loving, treasured child.

Cautioning him or her to be careful and good. Avoiding
dangerous places and peers, both bad and wild.

Abiding by our wishes and following our advice, attending
a party, movie, or function close to home.

Our whole world is shattered; its course is forever altered by the
knock of a stranger at our door or an unfamiliar voice on the phone.

Mr. and Mrs. Safe Secure Citizen, the impossible
has happened. I am sad to advise.

Your son or daughter died this night.

A victim of violence, of a senseless murder, without reason or
logic, I am sorry to say, and I can't begin to explain why.

As reality begins to set in, family, friends, relatives, and neighbors
are stricken by disbelief. Overwhelmed by sorrow and grief, ponder
what has happened, struggling to grasp why it did or how it could.

One familiar thought is painfully honest: What has happened to my child
could not be. Or so I thought and truly believed. IT IS IMPOSSIBLE;
IT DOESN'T HAPPEN IN MY NEIGHBORHOOD.

Ralph L. Myers June 18, 1995

Father of the murdered son, Tom Myers.
Murdered in our safe neighborhood, July 24, 1993

"Down Tonight"

I wrote and posted this poem on the Parents of
Murdered Children's "Forum of Hope" in August 2000
in response to one of the forum members.

This woman's daughter had been murdered, and at the time
she was posting on the POMC Forum, she was suffering from
cancer. Sadly, we lost track of her as she stopped posting not
long after that, and we felt her illness was probably terminal.

My poem "Down Tonight" was intended as a message of
hope and that it was okay for her to feel "down," not only
that particular night but any time she needed to.

Ralph L. Myers

Down Tonight"

CE, after reading your post, we are down tonight.

Your pain is our pain as we share your plight.

Lean on us; depend on us as you go through another night.

The depth of your depression is at an all-time low.

Imprisoned deep within the darkness of your soul.

Surrounded by anguish and pain that is yours,
the depths of which only you can know.

The hopelessness in your heart remains consistent with
your level of depression and emotional pain.

Seeking comfort and solace with us, from us, does help as we get
through this life, which I agree, as you have stated, is insane.

Your friend, Tom's dad—Ralph

Ralph L. Myers
August 19, 2000

"Pity Party"

This is another poem I wrote and dedicated to the "Forum of Hope" members after reading several posts that they were having a particularly bad day or night and were immersed in what one member described as a "pity party."

When a horrible occurrence takes place in one's life (such as losing a loved one to murder), I feel it is only natural and human nature to feel sorry for oneself and perhaps be mired down in a so-called "pity party." I am not sure anyone could survive a tragedy of such magnitude and profound consequences without feeling at least sometimes sorry for yourself.

Ralph L. Myers

Pity Party

I woke up this morning at 3 AM.

Another night of tossing and turning, thinking of you and what happened. Sad and angry, your murder took place; it shouldn't have happened. Life and living now seem to be a sham.

God, I feel so bad, helpless, and alone.

Lying here thinking, why did it happen? Why were you stolen, taken away from this life and us, your loved ones, and the refuge of a loving home?

The horrible thoughts that persist, my sorrow, heartbreak, tears, and pain.

Are released, a flood of overwhelming tears and emotions I do not understand, from which I cannot refrain.

Where can I go? Who will listen and genuinely understand the way that I feel? Are the words that I speak or how I react not self-pity? No, I am not having a pity party. I just want to try and understand—be understood.

Life often seems meaningless and difficult because of the uncontrollable and ever-changing mood. I can't go back to sleep, so I go to my computer and log onto this Forum, where I can safely talk of my sadness and despair.

Here, I can talk, cry, rant, and rave to all you other survivors. You know I do not seek pity; I just need to talk, express myself to you in a way that one like you has suffered, understands, and genuinely cares.

Ralph L. Myers
November 25, 2000

"Please Excuse my Rambling."

Once again, I wrote this poem in response to the postings of other survivors of murdered loved ones as they tried to express their feelings on the "Forum of Hope." As some indicated, they felt they were merely "rambling" when posting some of their personal feelings and thoughts.

Sometimes, we need to "ramble," and when you can do so in a place like the "Forum of Hope," where you are not criticized or judged by others who have suffered a loss like you have, I have to say it is very therapeutic and helpful in the grieving process.

Ralph L. Myers

"Please Excuse My Rambling"

Nearly every day, I visit this Topic Forum Page."

It appears it is the only place where I feel safe,
where I can truly rant and vent my rage.

Many times, I have read the thoughts of others as they express.

How their lives have become a horrible mess.

Filled with anger, grief, and stress.

Can anyone blame them, as they say?

How their lives have become a nightmare, a living hell.

Family and friends do not judge me for how I
feel, or say they understand my pain.

The murder of my loved one is impossible to accept, for I bear no blame.

While you truly cannot understand why I talk of them
whenever we meet, it's only because I love and miss them so
very much, and for feeling that way, there can be no shame.

So, my forum friends and confidants, I know you are
the only ones who understand, and when my posts are
long, please excuse and forgive me while I ramble.

Could it be because my life, like yours, has become a day-
to-day struggle, an attempt to cope, and my goal to
achieve is to merely get by and out of its shambles?

Ralph L. Myers
August 31, 2000

"Somehow I must go on."

It doesn't take a genius or Sigmund Freud to understand
that when terrible and stressful things happen in our
lives, we sometimes wonder how we can go on.

To survivors of murder victims who merely seek justice on behalf
of their murdered loved ones, it goes from wondering how we can
go on and instead becomes mandatory that we find a way and
resolve ourselves to the fact that "somehow I must go on."

Once more, I have written this poem because of things other
victim survivors have said on the "Forum of Hope."

Ralph L. Myers

Somehow, I Must Go On

Good morning, my precious one, I am faced with another day.

My life without you seems empty and shallow, without meaning
or hope, since you were stolen, forever taken away.

How can it be possible on such a beautiful, sunny, warm spring day?

Life has become so painful and complicated; an ominous
black storm cloud of grief seems to blanket my existence.
Is it ever going to pass, or is it here to stay?

Masses of people surround me, many I love and know, utterly impervious
to my heartbreak and pain. A life that has been reduced to a living hell.

How can I make them understand how I feel? Why has my
existence been imprisoned within an emotional shell?

I pray for guidance and strength; somehow, I must go on.

My message to the world is that an evil person has
someone who is loved and irreplaceably taken away.

I must, and I will, go on, depending on my POMC
Forum friends who will stay by my side.

Hopefully, they have also come to know, truly understand,
and most definitely need me. They also truly depend
on me. Please stay in touch. Don't go away.

Dedicated to all of us on the POMC topic forum.

Ralph L. Myers
June 13, 2000

Section III
Questioning

Questioning and Contemplating

"An irrational rationalization or an unjustifiable justification?"

I wrote this poem in December of 1995, nearly a year
after the trial of my son's murder. I was heavily involved
in the crime victims' rights movement at that time.

This poem deals with my observations and philosophy as I
questioned society in America, primarily when one examines
the opinions on the left and right of the political spectrum.

From a crime victim's vantage point, it is tough to understand the
rationalizations and justifications made in defense of people who commit
heinous acts and why they should not be held accountable for those acts,
no matter what minority or disadvantaged group they are or come from.

To me, those rationalizations are irrational, and
the justifications are unjustifiable.

Ralph L. Myers

An Irrational rationalization or an unjustifiable justification?

Today, society in this observer's mind appears to
take on a paradoxical, oxymoronic meaning.

Often, our deeds are immoral and corrupt, yet we are convinced and
preach the doctrine of their morality and righteousness according to
our own irrational rationalizations or unjustifiable justifications.

In their minds, many view themselves as disadvantaged and oppressed.
They convince themselves of irrational rationalization, or the unjustifiable
justification that taking advantage and oppression are proper and correct.

Suffering from physical and psychological abuse and neglect, irrational
rationalization, or the unjustifiable justification is further perpetuated
by additional acts of physical and mental abuse and neglect.

Taking another's life is irrationally rationalized and unjustifiably justified
because they are a part of a particular race, color, or creed. Yet all the
while, their victims and the loved ones they leave behind are told they
should have pity and empathy. That their loved one's murderers should
not be held accountable for the commission of their horrendous deeds.

Ethical and theological battle lines have been drawn between pro-
life and pro-choice combatants. Both sides resort to irrational
rationalizations and unjustifiable justifications to further their cause.
Even though many future mothers are battered and abused, those acts
of battering are often overlooked, tragically ignored, or excused.

Yes, life and society today seem to be paradoxical oxymorons, complete
with irrational rationalizations and unjustifiable justifications.

Ralph L. Myers

12/11/1995

"Better or Different?"

I also wrote this poem in December 1995 as I did a self-examination of my life as it had become since the murder of my son.

The conclusion I came to was that my life was not getting any better; it was just different. I think that anytime there is a life-altering tragedy in one's life, it is impossible for life to get better.

In the fourteen-plus years that have transpired since my son was murdered, I can agree with the thoughts expressed that we learn and progress after a tragedy, and perhaps in some ways, through the strengths and wisdom we gain, our resolve and dedication to a cause can help make other lives better. But to me, the only way my life would be better is for us to have our son back, alive, and happy with his own family.

Ralph L. Myers

Better or Different?

It has been said that fleeting moments of time act as healers. With time's passage, our pain and sorrow are lessened and eased. All things, good or bad, joyous or heartbreakingly sad, will pass by.

Their impressions are left only in our memories, as the passage of time acts like a magical potion, deadening our pain, as our saddened hearts are relieved.

All too often, scholarly people, schooled only in intellectual thinking or theory, void of actual knowledge or experience, tell us that the passage of time will serve as an elixir of healing, assuring us that our lives will get better as the loved ones we have tragically lost will become fond and treasured memories.

For all of us enduring the loss of a loved one to murder, we seek and pray that justice will be served. Those who commit such incomprehensible deeds are punished for their acts and no longer allowed to add further victims to society's murderous toll.

For those who it seems have no possibility of justice, because the persons responsible for taking their loved ones or friends are unknown and remain free, the passage of time may only be an anesthesia. Temporarily numbing and covering, yet never fully able to remove or alleviate their pain.

Better or Different (continued)

Alas, the passage of time, while to some it may seem "life will get better, " to those left behind to cope with our constantly changing moods and emotions, sorrows, and pain, hopefully, our lives will get better. Rather than as I currently feel, life has not gotten better; it has merely become different.

Ralph L. Myers

December 17, 1995

"Cognitive Journey of Dreams"

The human brain gives us the intellectual ability to reason, think, remember, dream, and act. Probably not a day goes by that those horrific acts and crimes, such as murder, are not committed. When I wrote this poem, I was questioning the cognizance in my mind and how any dreams my son, his mother, or I had for him were obliterated by his murder and changed them into nightmares.

Ralph L. Myers

Cognitive Journey of Dreams

Infinite time, limitless introspection is our course as we traverse uncharted byways of thoughts on our cognitive journey of dreams.

Roadblocks of emotions and circumstances of events, some only subconsciously recorded, while others are painfully experienced, all too horrible, atrociously arousing feelings of sorrow and pain. They become deeply ingrained agonies, drowning out our silent screams.

Onward as we go, dreaming of where we have been, and from whence we came, re-living significant moments of our lives. Events that have shaped our destiny, realizing that our course has been uncontrollably altered and will never again be the same.

Sometimes, our dreams are transferred into our nightmares, which may be more accurately described as trauma.

As traumatized, we have become by happenings beyond our control. We have loved ones violently lost as we continue on our cognitive journey of nightmares and dreams.

Ralph L. Myers

June 8, 1996

I wrote this poem while questioning the thoughts, theories, and opinions of those who subscribe to the belief that it is understandable and, yes, even acceptable when the bad elements in society commit horrible crimes simply because they were born into an underprivileged class. All too often, they are portrayed as the true victims of society by persons I have heard described as "victocrats" by a local Los Angeles talk show host, Larry Elder.

I find it very difficult, if not impossible, to rationalize or justify violent acts or crimes because of a person's race, creed, or color.

We live in America in the 21st Century, and while it is far from perfect, all people living here, whether they are citizens or non-citizens, are given an incredible opportunity, and I have to say that their life mold has been unalterably cast.

Ralph L. Myers

"Has Our Life's Mold Been Unalterably Cast?"

Theologians philosophically discuss. Sociologists debate and theorize about the reasons why, what, how, and why we are as we are. Did some omnipotent deity or social predetermination shape our lives, cast our plights into some unalterable mold?

Or can we rise above the consequences of life's conditions we were born into? By our race, ethnicity, religion, social, educational, or economic class that, through the chance of fate, controls our very existence, destiny as we traverse life's uncharted road?

Being born into a life of privilege, wealth, and unlimited opportunities is placed before some. Theirs for the taking, set on a pinnacle. Delicately balanced by a desire to succeed, a willingness to work, to achieve.

Their lives and accomplishments are seemingly guaranteed and poured into a mold that would appear unalterably cast as they are often led to believe.

Life's unknown events and uncontrollable experiences serve as a sculptor's chisel or a welder's torch, chiseling away or melting the perceptions and realities that our lives are cast into an unalterable mold.

Immeasurable lives are born into poverty, despair, or oppression. Are they doomed to be forever cast into an unalterable life's mold? A life of impoverished existence's bottomless pit of destitution and despair? Shackled with metaphoric chains of their oppressor's? Forced to bear a life of oppressive loads?

Giving homage to the allegiance that all are created equal. Each life at birth is cast into an unalterable mold and is merely a presumption of future life successes, failures, heartbreak, or joy. Caused by the accident of birth and the condition of life each is born into.

It is impossible to avoid or anticipate divine providence or fate. When one ponders the consequences of our actions, choices we freely or unwittingly make, our lives are not cast into unalterable molds. Our destinies can be altered, guided by hopes, dreams, and premises we strive for and aspire to.

Ralph L. Myers, January 1, 1998

"How can one explain?"

This poem I wrote is yet another attempt for me to question and understand, or at least to explain, the unexplainable murder of my son and the thousands of murders that occur every year in America.

To me, the bottom line is I don't think it can or ever will be explained to any survivor of a murdered loved one. It seems the best anyone can do is to try to theorize or rationalize violent acts, but how can one explain?

Ralph L. Myers

How Can One Explain?

Time passes by; life and living go on, how can one explain?

Some evil person, an evil deed, has taken away someone loved, ardently missed. Leaving only memories, tearing away a piece of your heart. As you ponder why? Experiencing unknowable emotional pain.

Lifetime friends and love can no longer reach out as they struggle with the brutal reality. Trying to understand, faced with their own and others' mortality, how can one respond? How can one explain?

Perhaps it was only moments, days, or maybe years since your nightmare began. The moment of the knock on your door, or when the telephone rang. Branding forever an indelible mark, a searing pain. The remaining part of your life is shrouded by sorrow, grief, and doubt. How can I, or how can one explain?

Hopefully, all our remaining tomorrows will be blessed with renewed hope and unexpected joys rather than condemned to a lifetime of sadness and sorrow. As we continue to endure, this has become our refrain. Ever seeking an answer to why, we may never be able to understand. So, how can one explain?

Ralph L. Myers
October 14, 1996

"Life's Experiences, Life's Questions"

I believe that the experiences each of us has as we grow from birth until we die influence our beliefs, attitudes, and philosophies. Those factors, added to the parenting you received or perhaps lack of, will in all probability shape you into the human being you turn out to be and how you are able to relate to other humans.

Fortunately, I was raised by a loving, religious two-parent family that instilled basic and decent values in me, as I tried to do with my children.

I still firmly believe that while your good and bad experiences definitely affect how you react and view life, I still can't excuse or accept behavior or criminal acts as being justified solely on them. It is with these thoughts in mind that I wrote this poem four years after the murder of our son.

Ralph L. Myers

Life's Experiences—
Life's Questions—Life's Philosophy

In the beginning, God created all living things

From the dust of the earth, He fashioned humankind,
molding and shaping us in His own image. We were
but clay, merely putty in His loving hands.

We were born into a world of uncertainty, as a woman or a man.

At birth again, we were merely putty, with Life being the artist,
shaping, sculpting, and controlling our destinies. Life is ever
evolving, posing unanswerable questions, and developing our
perceptions, our philosophy of who, what, and why we are.

Our mother and father, each a person and event we have come into
contact with, serve as "Life's Artist" paint brushes, giving shape, adding
color, meaning, and pathos as our journey through life continues to its
conclusion—its unassumingly, and often unexpected, untimely end.
"Artist Life's" paintbrush, with its bristles made up of our
experiences, prejudices, loves, desires, and insecurities, continues
to portray our lives as a masterpiece of achievements. Or an
illustration of disillusions and frivolity on its canvas made
of the sands of time's relentless, unstoppable passage.

Once, I was certain, confident, and self-assured of what life was all
about. Steadfastly self-convinced, only I could control who, what, and
why I am. Life's unexpected happenings, unforeseen, uncontrollable
events give cause and reason for a purposeful reconsideration,
examination, rhetorical, and philosophical self-evaluation.

Ralph L. Myers
May 4, 1997

Journey along life's road

"The Winds of Remembrance"

I wrote this poem while waiting for my flight back to Los Angeles, sitting at a restaurant at the Indianapolis airport where I was born.

The March winds were howling outside that day, and it was very cold. Sitting in the restaurant watching things being blown around at the airport, I penned these thoughts about my life and events leading up to that cold March day, comparing them metaphorically to the wind.

Ralph L. Myers

The Winds of Remembrance

Frigid and continuous are these March midwestern winds.

Freezing, chilling currents of air. Attracting like some invisible
magnetic force, memories of people and events long since passed.
Continuing a sporadic course is impossible to alter or rescind.

Time and fate have caused my return. I am rekindling
memories of my Indiana youth, and the winds of
remembrance press me ever onward on life's sojourn.

Carefree days, seasons of warmth, beauty, and cold. Pushed
continually forward by the winds of remembrance as our
youth fades into time that has passed. Accelerating through
all the future tomorrows as we age and grow older.

Thanks are due to God for his gift of love of a son, daughter,
and wife. Sharing in their love, the only true love of my life.

Extending before us a journey of love as father, mother, husband, and wife.

Gently, the winds of remembrance, with breezes, were blowing. As I think back on the birth of our children, memories of those blessed events have caused a place in our hearts to be warm and forever glowing.

The winds of remembrance are increasing at a speed
of joy and happiness, blessing our lives and creating
spiraling, whirling vortexes of circumstance.

A vacuum of sorrow created by a tornado of tragic loss and events gives cause to the winds of remembrance to create our desire to long for

The Winds of Remembrance (continued)

times forever past. Instead of living in all future tomorrows.

Our lives will continue to rush forward. While the winds of remembrance forever embrace our minds with loving thoughts, memories of those we know and knew, love and loved, as our time here can never be paused, never turned backward.

Ralph L. Myers

March 25, 1996

Written by Ralph Myers at the Indianapolis, Indiana International Airport after visiting his sick mother.

Swirling Vortex of Circumstances

"What is the Answer?"

I have referred to this section of my book of poems as "questioning" because even an uneventful life still poses many unanswerable questions.

The search for answers becomes even more profound when there is a loss of a loved one to murder. Many questions will never be answered in our lifetimes. I often can't even think of a logical question to ask.

In this poem, I have surmised based upon my perceptions and feelings that the answers we as survivors of murdered loved ones seek are elusive and perhaps unobtainable.

Ralph L. Myers

"What Is the Answer?"

Every wakening day, each conscious moment, we
search, we question, and we ponder why?

Hoping against all hope there must be, there should
be, and we deserve an answer, a reply.

Life and living have become so difficult. Shrouded by so many
doubts, so much grief, and so much pain. Where is relief?
Where does the solution to the elusive response lie?

Will it be, can it ever in this our time, granted here on earth, be explained
to the survivors why our loved ones were chosen to die before us?

As I sit here writing, philosophizing, seeking a
rationalization or explanation for what the answer is, I
have arrived at a premise rather than a conclusion.

Will we ever have an answer to our question, or is
the possibility for one merely an illusion?

Based upon our broken hearts, grounded by undeserved
loss and unwanted, unearned disillusion?

Ralph L. Myers
August 26, 2000

"Did you ever wonder why?"

I wrote this poem more as a rhetorical question and point of view. I did so after chatting with so many other survivors of murdered loved ones on the "Forum of Hope" site. I was trying to put into words my feelings and those of so many others about their lives, what they were confronted with, and how they are viewed by much of society now that they are survivors of murdered loved ones.

Writing this poem was therapeutic to me, and perhaps should be in Section V of this book under (Rage-us versus them.)

Ralph L. Myers

"Did You Ever Wonder Why?"

I thought I was a person of at least average intelligence, but I am beginning to wonder.

Have you ever wondered why life and living have become so complex and why there aren't many answers or solutions to our problems, only rationalizations and excuses?

Did you ever wonder why so many supposedly well-meaning persons are quick to defend brutal, murderous acts committed against all of society and somehow want to shift the blame for some inane reasons to those who have had these crimes committed against them?

Did you ever wonder why it is considered cruel and inhuman to execute a violent murderer and ignore the heinous indignities and cruelties that they inflicted upon their victims? Almost painlessly and clinically

Did you ever wonder why violent murderers seem to become cult heroes and their acts glamorized by our culture, captured by the mass media, and recorded for posterity of future generations, while those whom they murdered soon become nameless and forgotten as though they never existed?

Did you ever wonder why there are so many judges, politicians and organizations willing to fight for the rights of convicted murderers? But they do not seem to worry about even one innocent person being murdered. Even though every year countless persons whose only crimes were walking down the street, sleeping in their homes, attending church or working on their jobs are sent to their deaths without the benefit of legal representation, constitutional guarantees, appeals, or even a concern for any of those rights, do they have a due process?

Did you ever wonder why, during the trial of a person who was found guilty beyond a reasonable doubt, their attorney would employ any legal maneuver, dirty trick, or prevarication to ensure that their client would not be held accountable, while the victim or their survivors are always made to remain silent and without expression or emotion by the court?

Did you ever wonder why lifelong friends, family members, churches, and most of society will become impatient with you if you want to talk about your murdered loved one? Even indignant and hostile if you insist you want some considerations of justice being afforded, you like those that are being afforded to their murderers?

Did you ever wonder why you have been cast into the tragic position in life you now find yourself in? All the while trying to recover, grieve and make sense of the senseless?

If there is an answer to our rhetorical questions, did you ever wonder why it is at least elusive, perhaps unanswerable? Or just maybe the answers are so obvious and straightforward that many in an uncaring society really cannot see past their own political correctness, bias, and insensitivity towards crime victims or their survivors.

So, the question has changed from "did you ever wonder why" to simply WHY?

Ralph L. Myers
March 1, 2001

WHY?

In October of 2000, I wrote this poem. I dedicated it to a member of the POMC Forum who related the additional trauma and pain she suffered after her son was murdered. The police called her at work instead of telling her of the horrible loss in person. Since it is over the telephone, getting a call like this may initially seem like a very sick prank. What is truly needed by the survivors of a murdered loved one is a notification in person, and with a grief counselor in attendance with the police.

Having experienced being notified (at least in person) by the homicide detectives, I helped establish a crisis response team in the West Valley Division of the Los Angeles Police Department to assist the police when news of this nature must be advised to surviving family members and friends. The person(s) being notified needs additional assistance in what should be done next, i.e., contacting the coroner's office, making funeral arrangements, and helping in contacting other family members and friends.

Ralph L. Myers

"Did You Think?" ©

Mr. Police Officer, Policewoman, or Coroner, another
night of violence, another victim, another body, now
you must perform one more horrible task.

Your last duty before your watch ends is to notify the victim's
family, the father and mother, but before you do, you must pause.
What do you think? While for yourself, you must ask.

Here before me lies John or Jane Doe.

A person I never knew, how special they are or how much
they are loved, how I will ever explain such a horrible loss to
those they loved, they have been dealt life's cruelest blow.

Lord give me strength, compassion like that, which
was written in King David's Psalm.

With wisdom surpassing King Solomon, as I ponder my John
or Jane Doe, it is much more than that they are someone's
loving brother or sister, daughter, son, father, or mom.

Rather than make a telephone call, all they will remember they
heard was a strange, cold, uncaring voice on the phone.

I owe it to them that I will soon let you know this day your loved one
was murdered, I share this loss with you, and you are not alone.

As you blindly try to get by, survive, and get through.

I hope you are aware I cared as any human should, I performed my
horrible duty with feeling, sympathy as though Jane or John Doe
could have been one of my loved ones or someone I once knew.

Ralph L. Myers

October 29, 2000

*Dedicated to Marsha for the added pain she
experienced when she was uncaringly told of the
murder of her beloved son John on April 17, 1991*

Section IV
Observations

"Created Equally"

When I wrote this poem in November 1998, I realized that
theoretically, all people are created and born into this life equally.

We are born without sin and have a pure, snow-white slate
without marks or blemishes for our good or bad deeds.

It is a prayer that we live a good, guiltless, or sin-free life
as much as possible so that when our time is at its end, our
existence while living will be productive and good.

Ralph L. Myers

Created Equally

When we are born, each of us enters this life with souls
unblemished by thoughts, good or bad. Yet to commit acts
of compassion, unkindness, prejudice, greed, or hate.

Our lives, our existence, is stretched before us. Whose
sins of omission or commission have yet to be etched
on symbolic white marble or slate ledgers.

If there is original sin, as some believe, I also say there
must be original innocence. For at the time of birth,
we have not had a chance to sin or deceive.

Live out the time on this earth we are granted. Lives that
are tolerant just and wise. Giving no reason for our friends
or foes to have cause to question, doubt, or surmise.

When our time here on earth ends, our symbolic
ledgers are tallied, judged, and reviewed.

May God have given us guidance and directed our journeys
as we enter eternity with souls relieved and enlightened
due to our actions and how we lived and believed.

May our spirits be renewed.

Ralph L. Myers
November 9, 1998

"It's time I must leave. It's time I must go."

It had been less than two years since the murder of my son when I wrote this poem. To my parents, it sounded ominous, and they worried that perhaps I was thinking of committing suicide. Let me assure you, the reader, as heartbroken and devastated as I was, such a thought never entered my mind. I was driven to one final act of parenting for my son: to make certain his voice was heard, and he received justice.

I was expressing my thoughts and observations about
whether we existed in pre-life, and when we were born, that
was the "it's time I must leave, it's time I must go.

After we are born, each step or stage of our lives begins and ends, and
that is what I meant by "it's time I must leave, it's time I must go."

When we do reach the time when we are to leave this
life and go to an afterlife existence, then once more,
it is time I must leave; it's time I must go.

Ralph L. Myers

It's Time I Must Leave;
It's Time I Must Go

Existence in pre-time, and the immeasurable eons of eternity,
my living, breathing stay on this place called earth is but a
nearly invisible speck cast upon the dimension of actuality.

Allowed by God to be given to a father and mother
through a spiritual and physical act of love, I am destined
to be someone's daughter or son, sister or brother.

It is my time to be born. My body is ordained to unite with my soul. My
spiritual dwelling in pre-time is at an end. It's time I leave; it's time I go.

Newly born, naked and innocent, my infant mind was utterly
void of any pre-time existence, as I was placed in the arms of
my mother for love, protection, nurture, and subsistence.

The ticking seconds of time begin measuring the allotted span of this
life and all its joys and hopes, trials and tribulations that I will know.
They remind me that it's time I must leave; it's time I must go.

As I partake of the experiences of life cast before me as I traverse along
its road, time never pausing as events and my deeds only add to the
weight of its load. Pushing me ever onward, time refusing to slow, I am
compelled to remember: It's time I must leave; it's time I must go.

Unknowingly, unwillingly, as my time reaches its end,
reflecting back on what was accomplished or what might
or should have been, one equal lasting reality all others
presuppose, it's time I must leave, it's time I must go.

Ralph L. Myers
May 13, 1995

"Life's Experiences—
Life's Questions—Life's Philosophy"

I wrote this poem in one of my more reflective moods and countless observations I was attempting to make about life, its experiences, questions, and my personal philosophy.

As the reader of this poetry book can readily ascertain I was brought up by my parents with religious beliefs and after the murder of our son even though I do not regularly attend any church I have always maintained those beliefs. In fact, they helped me to survive the ordeal of losing my son to murder.

Ralph L. Myers

Life's Experiences—
Life's Questions—Life's Philosophy

In the beginning, God created all living things.

From the dust of the earth, He fashioned humankind,
molding and shaping us in His image. We were but
clay, merely putty in His loving hands.

Each of us was born into a world of uncertainty, as a woman or a man.

At birth again, we were merely putty, with Life being the artist,
shaping, sculpting, and controlling our destinies. Life is ever
evolving, posing unanswerable questions, and developing our
perceptions, our philosophy of who, what, and why we are.

Our mother and father, each a person and event we have encountered,
serve as "Life's Artist" paint brushes, giving shape, adding color,
meaning, and pathos as our journey through life continues to its
conclusion—its unassumingly, and often unexpected, untimely end.
"Artist Life's" paintbrush, with its bristles made up of our
experiences, prejudices, loves, desires, and insecurities, continues
to portray our lives as a masterpiece of achievements. Or an
illustration of disillusion and frivolity on its canvas made
of the sands of time's relentless, unstoppable passage.

Once, I was certain, confident, and self-assured of what life was all
about. Steadfastly self-convinced that only I could control who, what,
and why I am. Life's unexpected happenings, unforeseen, uncontrollable
events give cause and reason for a purposeful reconsideration,
examination, rhetorical, and philosophical self-evaluation.

Ralph L. Myers
May 4, 1997

"Look at This"

During one of the many sleepless nights, I suffered after the murder of my son, I got up at 3:30 AM to write down these thoughts that kept going through my mind.

I feel that the events or stages of each of our lives are metaphorically like pages in the book of our lives, each with a particular meaning or significance that, in the end, will define who we were and the kind of life we lived.

Ralph L. Myers

"Look at This"

Look at this, what you see is what you observe, is a page.

Deep from within our bosoms, torn from our
hearts, crumpled, and yellowed with age.

Look at this, each wrinkle, fold, and tear, concealing
our hopes, anger, pain, grief, and rage.

Look at this, a page torn asunder from the story of our lives, a
page part of a great novel with a blurred and vague beginning.

Filled with events and people loved and revered, plots and
sub-plots as the story unfolds, recklessly wandering along an
uncharted course, reaching its climactic, unimaginable ending.

Look at this, this weathered and fading page.

Torn from somewhere in this book of our life, whether
near the beginning, middle or end, can only be
surmised by God or some omnipotent sage.

Look at this. Without this torn page, this book of our lives
would have lost some of its meaning, reason, or adage.

Ralph L. Myers
April 3, 1995
3:30 AM

"Perceptually Intellectual"

Anyone who watches television, reads the newspapers, or listens to the radio, especially talk radio, will agree that we are constantly bombarded by people who have a particular agenda or espouse a left- or right-leaning political persuasion.

Being a surviving victim of a murdered loved one the awareness of these persons who are perceived to be the "last word" or intellectually elite becomes even more acute.

Since we live in a free society, it is desirable and indispensable that a wide range of viewpoints be discussed. As free persons, we have the right to form our own opinions about whatever the subject matter is.

However, my problem is with the so-called intellectually elite knowing what is best for all of us. If we disagree or express a different opinion from them, then we are uninformed, illiterate, or a left or right-wing radical.

I wrote this poem in June of 1996 just one month before the third anniversary of my son's murder as I examined and observed those who felt they were superior to the rest of us and intellectually elite when in reality they are or were the "perceptually intellectual."

Ralph L. Myers

Perceptually Intellectual

Genetically derived intelligence is enhanced and expanded
through education and experiences. We are influenced by our own
thoughts and evaluations, and we are perceptually intellectual.

Articulating precisely with grammatical clarity, convincing
rationalizations, and angst-driven insecurities and prejudices,
to many, we are deemed perceptually intellectual.

While all around us, they say we have erected a façade, a shield
against world calamities and life's realities, which they have reduced
to nothing more than mere unfortunate and tragic occurrences.

Meanwhile, because of our stations in life or our ability to create
an image of seemingly mental superiority, we are sometimes
judged to be or have become perceptually intellectual.

I ask, too, what good, or for what purpose, is being
perceptually intellectual, when by our actions and
through our deeds we only accomplish a lifetime of non-
accomplishments or social and moral inadequacies?

As my life progresses or when it has reached its end, I want to
be remembered as a caring individual, a man of actions and
worthy contributions, rather than only a learned individual,
labeled and thought of as perceptually intellectual.

Ralph L. Myers

June 14, 1996

"Placed on the Precipice of Time"

I wrote this poem just 15 months after the murder of my son, as I made a personal observation that life as we live is a journey and the road we take is like a precipice, whereas we go along its path, we do a balancing act so as not to fall off into an abyss.

Sometimes, no matter how careful we are, our lives are shattered because of the actions of others. We have no control over those actions and are pushed off the precipice into the abyss.

Ralph L. Myers

Placed on the Precipice of Time

When our spirits are united with our physical, earthly
being, they are borne onto The Precipice of Time.

The Sun, Moon, and Stars in the heavens above shine down on our
existence below, as we traverse life's journey along the Precipice of Time.

Each of us is driven by forces and circumstances beyond our control.
Towards a future and destiny unknown, we are held on the Precipice
of Time by a lifeline of love, strength of convictions, and all others
who share it with us. This lifeline is constantly in danger of being
severed by circumstances of thoughtless, cruel, and uncaring
actions done by mankind to their fellow man and woman.

While The Precipice of Time may be short for some, and
longer for others as they travel along its path. All who are
placed upon it will reach its end at the junction of the Sea of
Eternity, where once more their spirits will forever dwell.

Ralph L. Myers
October 22, 1994

"I'm in this place called here, and you are in that place known as there."

When a loved one dies and is taken away from those who knew and loved them, leaving them behind in the "here" they have traveled or gone to another dimension, which, for want of a better description, is referred to as "there."

When I wrote this poem in June 2000, I attempted to give here and there a meaning of what it meant to me and how I felt about my son leaving "here" and going to "there, "wherever "there may be.

Ralph L. Myers

I'm in this place called here,
and you're in that place
known as there."

Although our separation is due to the cruel, senseless act of another, I'm in this place called here, and you're in that place known as there.

Where is this place called here, and that place known as there?

Is here my physical presence on earth, and there my hope for a relief from my pain of losing you, the immeasurable depth of my sorrow and despair?

Can it be that here is a state of mind, and there the next plateau we reach?

If so, what words of wisdom are ours that we may teach?

To you, my precious one, the loss of you has caused an insurmountable void, a reason for many a tear.

Today, I remain with only a memory of you in this place called here, and you have journeyed to that place known as there.

In some future dimension, we will again be together in a place called forever. Rather than in this place called here, or that place known as there.

Ralph L. Myers
June 3, 2000

"Months on the Calendar"

This is probably the lengthiest poem I have written, and I did so and dedicated it to all the other survivors of murder victims in honor of the month when their loved one was murdered.

Murder and heartbreak do not skip any month, and each month on the calendar has a significant meaning for the season it falls within.

Ralph L. Myers

"Months on the Calendar"

The sound of ticking clocks and the syncopated beating of our hearts mark and measure the sounds of our lives. Our very existence is recorded on this date. Entries are made in a journal of time recorded on the pages of the months on the calendar.

Each entry tells a story of our lives. Some are insignificant, some joyful, or some incomprehensibly horrible and sad.

To those who have suffered the loss of a loved one to murder. A loss that, like any other, is impossible to compare. Bringing back memories too painful as I sit at this place, looking at this date marked on this calendar. With thoughts spinning through my memory, it seems like an engine that is racing in neutral gear, rapidly going nowhere.

January

It was during the stark coldness of January
when you were brutally taken away.

A frigid, numbing feeling of loss took possession of my soul on that day.

February

The shortened month of February, when you were
forced to go away, this earthly place leaves.

As your family and friends were left behind with broken hearts to grieve.

March

March is upon us, a promise of the renewal of life. The
appearance of spring's first Robin gave us a glimmer of hope.

But it was replaced by despair and sorrow when you
were stolen away. Leaving us only with thoughts of
survival and how, oh, how would we cope?

April

The showers on that day in April could not keep pace
with the realization and horror that your life had ended,
with the cascading flood of tears taking their place.

May

The warmth of May's sun, fields, and meadows of flowers all around
us in colorful, vibrant, and spectacular bloom could not comfort us or
diminish our sadness when your life was taken on that day in May.

A month honoring Mothers instead will always be
remembered as a month when the joy of motherhood
was overshadowed by their pain and gloom.

June

The weddings, school graduations, and Father's Day celebrations
of the first month of summer, as this calendar reaches June.

When you were murdered, our lives became devastated, dark,
and bleak like a night that is void of any stars or moon.

July

As we mark this commemoration, an observance of the
birth of our nation during this month of July.

Instead, we are in mourning as we struggle to understand. Grasping for a
reason why, on that day, you were called to your heavenly home on high

August

The August dog days of summer are bringing torrid heat,
depriving us of any relief from a gentle cooling rain.

You are gone; you were taken, leaving all that loved you behind,
our souls being scorched with a searing, burning pain.

September

September's harvest, as the brightness of the sunny summer
days is shorter, seems to serve as a metaphor for the end of
your life by an agent of death, the unholy harvester.

October

With its beauty of falling leaves in an October canvas of fall
colors, Autumn was transformed into shades of black and
gray when you were lost, replaced by death's pallor.

November

November, when you were so needlessly taken away, was
transformed from a month of Thanksgiving.

Now we observe it with reluctance, pain, and disdainful misgiving.

December

December, the last month of the year, as marked on this calendar, is
the joyous season of giving, peace on earth, and goodwill to all.

This special meaning no longer has meaning to us when,
through the violent act of another, you answer God's call.

Ralph L. Myers
June 26, 2000

"No Reason, No Why"

On the 7th anniversary of the murder of my son, I wrote this poem as I thought about a reason or a why such horrible things happen and how we are brought up to deal with them, particularly if you are a man.

Being heavily involved with the crime victims' rights movement, I felt we must take a stand against violence and try to make our case that there can be no legitimate reason for violence and murder to occur, only a question of why.

Ralph L. Myers

"No Reason, No Why"

It has been said, "ours is not to reason why."

Could that be because murder is indefensible,
without reason, or lacking a why?

As a young boy, I was told, Men don't cry.

If they show weakness and vulnerability, they
must hide their emotions and live a lie.

Invulnerable, emotionless, "ours is to do or die"

Forget, forgive, our hand has been dealt, fate cast
to unknown circumstances on high.

Instead, we must give a reason. We must state why.

Survivors must insist that the murder of our loved ones
must not be forgotten, that acts of violence committed
against them are deemed unforgivable, and that is our plea,
our reason for giving sound to their silenced reply.

For us not to question seeking a reason why to take
a stand against violence, then surely, through silence,
it will be cause for many more to die.

Ralph L. Myers
July 24, 2000
(The 7th anniversary of Tom Myers' murder)

"Oh, to be able to rewind."

While it is impossible and wishful thinking, I nevertheless thought about and wished that somehow our lives could be rewound so we could view and edit out the mistakes and tragedies that occur. With this fantasy thought in mind, I wrote this poem in August of 2000.

Ralph L. Myers

"Oh, to Be Able to Rewind"

Through the wonders of today's video and computer technology, we can save, edit, and delete events and moments of our lives, even pausing on recorded memories to cause reflective thoughts. This permits a sorrowful and often doubting, questioning "what if" mentality.

Of life and living as it once was, when we did not need to live using mind-altering drugs, grief counseling, or psychology.

If only we could fast forward past, rewind, or especially erase, horrible times, tragic events that none of our loved ones should have experienced or had never taken place.

Oh, if only we could rewind using some magical remote or other type of controls.

To happier times, bringing back murdered loved ones to be with us again, recording happenings of the present, instead of praying to God that justice in their names will indeed be served, as He protects and nourishes in heaven their arriving souls.

Ralph L. Myers
August 30, 2000

"Shadows we cast, marks that are left."

I wrote and dedicated this poem in the name of my newer friends in the victim's rights community for their efforts in seeking legislation for tough on crime and criminals, as well as the compassion offered by the grief support groups, such as Parents of Murdered Children, that are there for us.

I sincerely want and hope that the shadow of my life that I lived will cast a positive mark on posterity and that I will be remembered as a person that genuinely cared and wanted to help all future crime victims in their seek for justice either for themselves or in the name and memory of their murdered loved one. Ralph L. Myers

Shadows we cast.
Marks that are left

Vividly clear, precise images are the Shadows
we cast on life's bright sunny days.

Yet, the shadows we cast rapidly disappear, evaporating into a mist of
uncertainty, when dark foreboding clouds of circumstances and events
hover over our existence as though they are plots from a tragic play.

Those shadows we cast can't be sustained.

Only will our time allotted on this earth be recorded for future
generations to reflect on by the marks that we leave, murder
victim survivors, as we seek to play a part in easing and preventing
all victims of tomorrow suffering and emotional pain.

When our time, our life, has ended, we stand before eternity's bar,
and He tallies our evil and good deeds as we enter heaven, once again
to be united with our loved ones on that great spiritual plane.

I hope, I pray, that I was among those who will be able to
answer to God for humanity, compassion, and dignity of life
for all I tried, holding those who are evil accountable for their
deeds. I took a stand; I was determined, and I cared.

Will the shadows we cast, and the meager marks we left behind,
perpetuate an accurate actuality of compassion, equality, and
justice that was beyond reproach, beyond compare?

Ralph L. Myers,
November 15, 2000

"T' is the Season to be"

The Christmas holiday season is particularly difficult in our family because my son's birthday is just four days after Christmas, December 29th, and his sister's birthday is on Christmas Day.

As you might expect, this time of year was especially joyous and significant to us. While we still celebrate and enjoy Christmas, it just isn't the same without our son with us.

I wrote "T's the Season to be" just a few days before Christmas in 2000, thinking about the joyous holidays of the past and the less happy ones of the present.

Ralph L. Myers

"'T' is The Season to be..."

With another year gone by, another holiday season upon
us, White Christmas dreams, visions of sugarplums
that once danced in our heads, gatherings of family and
friends now seem to be replaced by stress and fuss.

As impossible as it may seem, the horror of losing you overshadows
my existence during this "T's the season to be jolly."

While memories of you may all be too painful and sad, losing you the
way we did instead makes this "T 's the season to feel melancholy."

I pray that I will be given the strength to endure and remember
the happier times we shared during the past holidays.

It will bring comfort and peace, soothing my pain through an elixir of
memories of you and times that I wish would or could have forever last.

Ralph L. Myers
December 15, 2000

"The Parable of the Victim"

When I wrote this it was meant more to be an essay than a poem
about the plight of the surviving victims of murdered loved ones
and being Christian, I used the Parables of Jesus as found in
the New Testament to illustrate their newly found position in
life and as they are viewed by society in many instances.

Ralph L. Myers

The Parable of the Victim

To those of the Christian faith, Jesus would teach his word to others through a story called a parable. Today, words of wisdom such as His teachings in the biblical times of the New Testament can be compared to metaphors, paradoxes, or analogies. His teachings were profound and are made readily understandable to nearly all levels of mental comprehension.

Except for the parable of the "Good Samaritan," which told about a victim of a robber on the highway and his need for help, I do not recall another example of a victim or survivor's plight.

The plight of victims and victimization in these days of the present differ only from the times past due to the vastness of numbers, horrific nature, and methods used to wreak havoc and heartbreak on those left behind.

What victim survivors of homicide victims go through is a classic example for the need of a parable so non-victims can perhaps in part understand us like the one I offer.

"The Parable"

In this time of violence, there seems to be no limit to the depth or scale of mankind's inhumanity to their fellow human being, as an ever-increasing multitude of victim survivors stand before civilization as testimony to this.

Parents, grandparents, children, relatives, or friends of those who have been lost due to this enigma of hatred and violence seek merely relief from their pain. That they will receive hope and an expectation that, in the memory of their lost loved ones, there will be an imposition of justice. The same expectation is unquestionably and unhesitatingly offered to those who have committed the horrific deeds against them.

To the media, hear our voices as they are now the pleas of our silenced loved ones. Report accurately on how our feelings of despair, fear, and distrust have become overwhelming and consuming passions and obsessions in our lives. Do not try to judge us or hypothesize on what our true feelings are. Please do not attempt to advise us. Do not tell us what our lives have or must now become. Most of all, do not make excuses or rationalizations in defense of the actions of the murderers who took our loved ones from us.

We call upon those in the justice system to realize that while "Lady Justice" is supposed to be blind, she is not to be rendered biased or deaf. Do not put our murdered loved ones on trial, for they are unable to speak out on their own behalf. The lack of their voices deafens true justice. Do not prevent their voices from being heard through their surviving loved ones by keeping them out of the courtroom or participating in the trial process. For their murderer, a right is guaranteed to a fair and impartial trial, and the tactic of preventing their survivors from being present truly gives credence that their trial is partial and unfair. That their victims never existed or are not painfully missed.

To the religious institutions and all those that have not been personally sinned against, as we have done, do not sit in judgment of us. If it is in our hearts to forgive, we will do so. If it is not, that is strictly between God and us. Do not expect us to continue living like nothing has happened, because the worst has. We are trying our best to cope with our loss, and there is no "one size fits all" method of coping.

The underlying method of this "Parable of the Victim" is that we merely ask and rightfully deserve patience, understanding, love, equal justice, and compassion, traits that were not shown or even considered for our murdered loved ones by their murderers.

Ralph L. Myers
June 10, 2000

"Doing Without"

This poem signifies that as we grow up, our parents teach us that it is impossible for us to have or get everything we would like to in life. In fact, we were also taught that it was a good thing to do without.

However, as my poem states and its underlying message suggests, there are, of course, some things that it is not good "doing without."

Ralph L. Myers

"Doing Without"

When we were young, we were told that doing without
is one of life's worthy sacrifices, a lesson of life taught
by someone with wisdom and words of gold.

As I now look back on a life careening ever so fast, I occasionally sit
and ponder, questioning those lessons taught many years past.

Were they lessons of truth or contradictions of thought?

Perhaps there are times when doing without was not necessarily
good. What could life have been like if doing so were for naught?

If we were doing without love, would there only be hate?

Without freedom, would our destinies be merely an
insignificant whim, controlled by the state?

Doing without justice in the name of those lost, so loved, so missed

Does that mean they did not matter, silenced voices, as though
they never lived, their lives seemingly dismissed by society?

Doing without you, a void has been created in my heart, a space.

Since I am now unable to console you or no longer able to embrace,
or feel the warmth of your love, wiping away a tear from your face.

Doing without hope, which was replaced by sadness
and despair, I struggle to survive, merely coping.

Doing without joy, would there only be sorrow and pain?

As we attempt to put shattered, devastated lives back
together again, will our efforts only be in vain?

For us, our kind of doing without is not what we were taught,
nor is it something good, as we were led to believe.

Rather than doing life as it was given, with you still
in our presence, is really all we could ever ask.

Ralph L. Myers
May 16, 2001

"Paradox of Society"

Although it is only my opinion based upon what I have been taught, learned, or experienced in life so far, I can only conclude that many of the problems we encounter in our daily lives are our own fault because many people are unwilling to hold people accountable for their deeds unless they fit into their social or political agendas.

Ralph L. Myers

"Paradox of Society"

Life is replete with its many contradictions.

Is it then so unusual to wonder or question its many rationalizations?

When one is convicted of a crime, why is it said
that society has a debt they must pay?

As it turns out, society actually "foots the bill"
for their crimes and wayward ways.

Someone once wrote, "crime does not pay."

But all one must do is look around, merely observe lawyers,
publishers, government agencies, entertainment media, and
institutions devoted to crime and criminal acts every day.

The promise of equal justice to be served for one and all is the
cornerstone of our freedom, an old rather than a new concept.

Why are those who have been afforded all their rights, found guilty
beyond a reasonable doubt by a preponderance of irrefutable evidence,
still defended and not held accountable by various groups and the ACLU?

Government programs were developed, and "professional think
tanks" were employed to discover the reasons for society's ills.

While decency and consideration for humanity are lauded,
a call for the return of moral concepts is dismissed as a
violation of rights and looked upon as a poison pill.

Of loved ones lost, victims of the Paradox of Society.

Causing sorrow and pain, and a lifetime filled with grief and anxiety.

Ralph L. Myers
May 19, 2001

Section V
Rage, us versus them.

"Circumstances of Victims"

I wrote this poem nearly two years after the murder of my son. By that time, my wife, daughter, and I had gone through the trial and sentencing for his murder. This poem was written and placed in this section dealing with the rage that survivors of murdered loved ones feel because, without fail, those observers on the outside will say our loved ones were a victim of circumstances and were in the wrong place at the wrong time. To me, for most incidents involving murder, the victims were not only in the place they should have been; it was the murderers who were in the wrong place at the wrong time.

Ralph L. Myers

Circumstances of Victims

Often it is said, yet another victim lies dead. Nearly all seem to agree that at the wrong place and time, they happened to be a victim of circumstances.

How else does one explain such tragedy, grief, and pain?

But is it true? As the loved ones they leave behind, they experience boundless feelings of shock and utter disbelief.

Seeking an answer to why? They continue to pursue.

No, I emphatically must conclude! A victim of circumstances, our loved ones were not. Their lives were too short. They were loved; they were good.

Instead, all should ponder the circumstances of victims, and why their lives were taken without reason or logic, their loving presence from their family and friends torn asunder.

The circumstances of victims matter not what race, creed, color, social, financial, or gender they were of, this is sure, those of us left behind, living without them, we are forced to endure.

Ralph L. Myers
May 29, 1995

"How do you plead, and your Victim, how did they?"

Anytime one must go before a judge for an infraction as insignificant as a traffic citation or as damning as being charged with murder they are asked how they plead, guilty, not guilty or no contest.

Something that has angered me a great deal since the murder of my son is the idea that the violent criminals in our midst are given every consideration in the criminal justice system so that they are treated fairly and receive all the constitutional rights they are entitled to.

Let me add, I don't disagree with those rights, it just angers me when I think of how their victims probably pleaded with them before they were brutalized and then murdered in a lot of cases.

It is with this anger in my mind that prompted me to write this poem.

Ralph L. Myers

How do you plead, and your Victim, how did they?

Evil, one vile and corrupt, you stand before this court of final resort,
being found guilty as charged for the taking of another's life.

An act so despicable, callous, and cold, causing infinite sorrow and pain
to be cast upon those left behind. Their lives are shattered and destroyed,
ensuring that their existence remains filled with anguish and strife.

For what you have done and before final judgment is passed,
how do you plead, and your victim, how did they?

Standing before eternity's bar begging for compassion, mercy, and justice
is your God-given right. In a trembling voice, I believe you are about to
say, "Go ahead, how do you plead, and your victim, how did they?"

Before you so brutally extinguished their life, did they not also beg
for compassion and mercy, pleading that they be allowed to continue
to love and continue to live, as you are now doing on this very day?

Please tell me again how you plead, and your victim, how did they?

Your day of judgment and reckoning is at hand.

Finally, you are accountable, and for all the tomorrows of forever,
you are doomed to remember one final question and reprimand.

How do you plead, and your victims, how did they?

Ralph L. Myers
April 10, 1996

"The Seemingly Forgotten"

The trial of our son's murderer had just ended when the "trial of the century" for O.J. Simpson began. Having just gone through a trial as a parent of a murdered child, just like the Brown and Goldman family was now going through, brought back painful and raw emotions, as all too often, the names of the victims are seemingly forgotten in the trial process.

I wrote this poem and sent it to both families, and said my prayers are with them. Sadly, in their case, the person charged, I feel, literally got away with murder, and there was no justice received by Nicole Brown, Ronald Goldman, or their families.

Ralph L. Myers

The Seemingly Forgotten

Numerous days and a vast number of hours of testimony
as the trial of the century continued to unfold.

Continuing to depict facts of horror and heartbreaking sorrow,
forced upon the families and survivors as the events of that fateful
June night, as witness upon witness, their attorney prodded
answers to questions are skillfully guided, repeated, and told.

The Seemingly Forgotten: the lives and existence,
hopes, dreams, and names of Ron or Nicole.

A "search for the truth" we constantly hear, when that very truth is cast
before our eyes, the lives of two loving persons brutally ended. Why and
for what possible reason we may not and probably won't ever know.

The Seemingly Forgotten by journalists and scholarly
pundits are the victims, Ron, and Nicole.

Each leaves behind a legacy of love, caring for others,
deeds, and unexpressed thoughts, though it often appears
they are like other victims. The Seemingly Forgotten are
emblazoned in our hearts and impressed upon our souls.

No, they are not seemingly forgotten; instead, they are the loved
and remembered, as we remember, capturing a cherished memory of
their past and a guiding path in our future, are Ron and Nicole.

Forever sons and brothers, daughters, sisters, mothers, relatives, or
friends, their lives serve as shining beacons, and our memories of them
must always remain as a reminder that they are not the Seemingly
Forgotten. Their shortened lives have taken an ungodly toll.

Ralph L. Myers
September 20, 1995
This poem is dedicated in the memory of
Ronald Goldman and Nicole Brown.

"A Mother's Wail"

I can't conceal my anger and contempt for those who are against the death penalty because they feel it is cruel and unusual punishment. Those people and/or organizations don't care about the horror, suffering, and the evil and unusual punishment inflicted upon their victims by those who are executed.

While I do have empathy for any mother whose son or daughter
is executed, their pain and suffering is no worse than the
mother who wails when the police come to the door to notify
her that her precious, loving child has been murdered.

Ralph L. Myers

"A Mother's Wail"

A mournful cry, a piercing shriek, sounds that could only be
created by Satan himself from the darkest region of Hell, that
sound we are told is what a mother makes, her painful wail.

As she powerlessly stands by when her son, who has
murdered another, pays the ultimate price as he ceases
to be inside the walls of some distant jail.

Capital punishment is barbaric, unjust, cruel, and insane. It is argued
that for the State to execute, to take another life is inhumane.

Even after years of appeals and delay.

Irrefutable, corroborating evidence is presented again and
again, yet for their murderous, unspeakable acts, the voices
are many and wrong when accountability is dismissed as
lawyers and organizations beg for yet another stay.

Unheard, overlooked, and ignored are the wails of the victim's mother.

For she was deprived of saying a final goodbye when the life of her
child was brutally ended by another, or the horror of discovering
the atrocity and violence done to her son or daughter.

Left in pain to die alone without the benefit or comfort of a
spiritual advisor or a mother crying out in a silenced wail in a
manner or by a means of a cruel act, a commission of slaughter.

No, nothing can be compared, nor is there anything more horrible than
the wail of a mother who, through violence, has lost a child to murder.

Nor is any concern about the suffering, horror, and pain inflicted upon
the victim rendered by the mother as she wails as her murderous, guilty
son is executed, crying out that his execution is cruel and inhumane.

Ralph L. Myers
October 19, 2000

"For them you were not there"

Again, I have only contempt and anger for persons that use any rationalization or excuses to try and halt the execution of a condemned murderer who has probably received several years of due process when their day of reckoning does finally arrive.

No such process, legal representation or even spiritual presence did they give their victims.

Ralph L. Myers

"For Them You Were Not There"

It was a warm, balmy Texas night.

Hundreds of protesters gathered around Huntsville prison to protest
a murderer's execution, claiming it was unfair and not right.

Nearly twenty years of appeals, legal maneuvers, and courtroom battles
all the way to the US Supreme Court carried Gary Graham's fight.

Calling his execution a state-sanctioned murder, cries of
outrage that justice was not served on this summer night.

Reverends Jesse and Al were in the execution chamber,
accompanied by an Amnesty International gal.

Expressing their outrage, saying the system was
wrong, the murderer was the victim now.

As all this unfolds at that Huntsville place.

Somewhere else, an actual innocent victim has been
murdered, forced to meet their maker face to face.

Stabbed, beaten, shot or raped, taken from their loved ones in less than
a heartbeat, their lives were ended, it mattered not what was their race.

They were executed without compassion, consideration, or the assistance of an attorney present to plead their case.

Sentenced and sent to eternity without the benefit of an appeal, their souls have been dispatched post-haste.

To all those protestors, I, as a survivor of a murder victim, to you I say "For Them You Were Not There" is an indictment that your outcry is wrong, your social priorities are an insult to the truly innocent victims, I feel I must vehemently state.

This poem is dedicated to the actual victims of society, our murdered loved ones.

Ralph L. Myers June 22, 2000

"Forgive"

One of the most challenging issues a survivor of a murder victim often faces is that they are asked if they will forgive their loved one's murderer. Or they are told they must or should do so by any number of persons, clergy members, or misguided friends.

It has been fourteen years since the murder of my son, and while I haven't ruled out the possibility that I will forgive his murderer, I think it is highly unlikely, and it is between my conscience and God, no one else!

If a victim survivor wants to forgive the murderer of their loved one, I do not think that is wrong, and they should do it. I don't want to be told what I should do.

Ralph L. Myers

"Forgive"

You ask us to forgive when what has happened
to our loved ones is unforgivable.

You say I should get over it, get on with my life,
when that life often seems unlivable.

Unable to forgive, we are told we have nothing to gain.

Yet try as we may, nothing seems to ease the heartbreak or pain.

I say to you, minister, priest, rabbi, or well-meaning friend.

Please spare me your sermon; let me deal with my own private God, and
perhaps someday, I will be able to transcend the anguish and sorrow.

Ralph L. Myers

May 25, 2000

*In July 2018, I forgave my son Tom's murder at a parole
hearing. This is something I must do if I follow the Lord's
commandments about forgiving and forgiveness.*

"Insane"

I wrote and posted this poem on the Forum of Hope site after
reading comments of other survivors of murdered loved ones,
who said they thought they were losing their sanity.

Sadly, losing someone to murder does cause severe mental and physical
illnesses in many people and even leads to their death all too frequently.

To any survivor of a murder victim who may read this book
of poetry and this poem in particular, if you feel you are
going insane, please seek the help of a grief counselor or a
support group such as Parents of Murdered Children.

Ralph L. Myers

"Insane"

Pervasive sadness, obsessive thoughts, depression out of control since
you were murdered seems to have taken possession of my physical
and spiritual being, my heart forever broken, my soul being branded
by an indelible mark, an unexpected, undeserved constant refrain.

As day after day and night upon night go by, I continue
to exist, consumed by seemingly unbearable pain.

Searching, questioning, and grasping for answers as to why
this burden was cast upon me gives me reason to doubt my
sanity. Surely, I must be going or have gone insane.

What was done to you, my precious one, was a cold, brutal
act of destruction, the ultimate act of cruel insanity.

It was done for you and me, a sin committed
against the entirety of humanity.

So, as it now seems to me that I stand on the
precipice of life, on the brink of insanity.

The taking of your life has forever exceeded the limits
of society and is an act of uncaring profanity.

Written by Ralph L. Myers
September 29, 2000

"Obsessed"

Many times, the passions and energies of individuals are construed by others as being obsessions. While this may be true in people who are diagnosed as being compulsive or obsessive, it is wrong to assume that survivors of murder victims are obsessive when they fight for justice in the name of their murdered loved one.

In this poem, "Obsessed," I tried to express my thoughts about what may be perceived by outsiders as an obsessed person.

Ralph L. Myers

"Obsessed"

Before our loved ones were murdered, they were
in our lives, and for this we were blessed.

Robbed of their love, their presence, and voices
silenced by murder and repressed.

We, the survivors, left behind to cope; to deal, admonished by
family, friends, and yes, even strangers, too. Get on with our
lives, get over it, do not allow yourselves to become obsessed.

Yearning, seeking, and expecting justice on behalf of our loved ones may
seem to those who have not lost are not affected to be an obsession.

Who are they to say, or how are they to know whether our
perceived obsession is our search for justice? Or has it become our
passion, or a dominating, overwhelming love and dedication?

Do not be so quick to judge a survivor.

Or their desire in the name and memory of their murdered
loved one, receiving some form of justice, is begrudged.

May circumstances never cast you into such a horrible
condition or state when your love and dedication are mistaken
as obsession and subjected to meaningless debate.

Ralph L. Myers

August 24, 2000

"Right Place, Right Time"

I wrote this poem on the eve of the 7th anniversary of the murder of my son. He was at a private party for one of his friends who had joined the military service. He was where he belonged, at the right place and time.

Whenever I hear people, for whatever reason, try to rationalize the murder of a person by saying they were in the wrong place at the wrong time, it bothers not only me but most survivors of murder victims.

In my poem "Right Place, Right Time," I have tried to present the viewpoint of the victim-survivor.

Ralph L. Myers

Right Place, Right Time

It was on the news today, reporting to all that
their life by murder had been taken.

The police came to our door today with the news that has turned our
world upside down; our lives have been forever changed and shaken.

We need to understand, cope, and explain as
neighbors, family, friends, and even strangers.

Your murder, while tragic and senseless, as it seems to
have been, most assuredly was pre-ordained.

Comments made about this tragedy are nearly without exception.

They were in the wrong place at the wrong time; their
common misconception is rationalization.

But wait, think for a moment. How could that be? Was it the wrong
place, wrong time? They were in their home, soundly asleep.

When an intruder broke in and decided their
life was theirs to take, to keep.

Or was it at school, work, or church, places where they belong
when their life was so cruelly and unnecessarily ended?

Or a party at the home of a friend, which they attended?

No, they were where they belonged, and at the
right place and at the right time.

So please think about it and realize our murdered loved
ones, victims of murder, the most heinous crime.

It was not they but their murderer who was at
the wrong place at the wrong time.

Ralph L. Myers
July 23, 2000

"Victim—Victimized"

In this poem, I have written about the feelings and
opinions of the survivors of murdered loved ones.

We are victimized when they become merely a statistic and
their lives and the kind of people they had been are soon
forgotten; in fact, they become the property of the State
that prosecutes their murderer if one is apprehended.

Ralph L. Myers

"Victim, Victimized"

On that sad, sad, and most horrible day, the day
you were murdered and stolen away.

To society, you became a statistic, just another victim,
and we who are left behind are victimized.

Throughout the investigation and arrest, if there indeed was one.

The meaning of your life was soon forgotten, for you no
longer existed, another victim you had become.

Yes, merely another victim, and we are victimized,
suffering a loss second to none.

As unbelievable as it may seem to some, when you were
murdered, you suffered life's most horrible fate.

You no longer exist except as a victim, victimized, we were, as
you simply became property of the people of the state.

For those of us considered fortunate that the murderer was caught,
tried, and convicted, we have received justice, or so it is surmised.

We can now get on with our lives, forget about
them, and how we have been victimized.

Now, it would seem that reaching out to each other in a place, a forum
where others freely speak out, eases our pain and gives us hope.

As we speak in anger, we sometimes express our
pain and despair as we try to cope.

Those very thoughts and emotional expressions we are told to limit
as they too become victims, and our right to express is victimized.

Ralph L. Myers
July 14, 2001

"Then maybe we could get over it."

Another thing that is all too often told to a survivor of a
murder victim by supposedly well-meaning family members
and friends is to "get over it and get on with your life."

If only it were that easy. I wrote this poem for those on the
outside, hoping that telling survivors they must get on with
their lives is insensitive and hurtful. I can assure you they are
getting on with their lives in the best manner they can.

Ralph L. Myers

"Then Maybe We Could Get Over It"

My dear misguided family member or friend.

I want to believe your words are sincere, your
intentions are good, and you truly mean well.

As you observe from the outside, my life has
been transformed into a living hell.

The words you have spoken are meant to be comforting advice.

Get over it; get on with your life. God, how I wish that I could
explain, especially to myself. Searching for an answer to help me
understand something, I would gladly welcome an explanation. The
explanation would then perhaps soothe my pain and suffice.

If only I could turn back time before that terrible day.

Prevent what happened, or at least one more time tell you I love you
and say a final goodbye before you were so senselessly stolen away.

Rebuild our shattered lives, allowing us to once more be a part of a
normal, loving family or supportive and understanding friend.

As we try to survive and cope searching for an existence with
our present unwanted conditions of life that were cast upon us
causing pain and heartbreak that seems like it will never end.

Please give us the strength to persevere.

Shielding all others, too, whose lives have been shattered, all normalcy destroyed, as now the murdered ones they so loved are forever taken away, may God soothe and repair their broken hearts.

As the new unknown challenges, we are forced to confront, as a murdered loved one's survivor is thrown in our path with the dawning of each new day. Why must we be constantly admonished to forgive and forget?

If only those on the outside looking in supported us more and judged us less, then and only then could we maybe get over it.

Ralph L. Myers
February 15, 2001

Section VI
Acceptance and Realization

"Our Organization of Sorrow."

For a mother, father, sister, brother, aunt, uncle, grandmother, grandfather, other family members or friends, and the entire community of a murder victim, in all honesty, there can never be acceptance of losing someone to violence. This is why I have only written one poem in this section. It is dedicated to organizations such as Parents of Murdered Children and Other Survivors of Homicide because, as a survivor of a murder victim, you are accepted into this group. There are no forms or applications to complete, no membership committees to see if you meet the criteria to be a member, just heartfelt sorrow and acceptance.

Ralph L. Myers

Our Organization of Sorrow

Another month, yes, another meeting, our leader
calls to order Our Organization of Sorrow.

Loved ones lost, stolen away from those in attendance,
comprising our Organization of Sorrow.

With pain and heartache, we welcome new members
who join us in our Organization of Sorrow.

Overcome by our grief, telling of unfathomable deeds of cruelty
and horror, seeking comfort and solace from the understanding
and loving care of Our Organization of Sorrow.

Daily, as we exist, challenging our faith, testing our resolve,
continuing our search for a quenching, healing relief from our pain,
we have through circumstances not of our imagination or choosing
to become intimately entwined in Our Organization of Sorrow.

This poem is dedicated to the surviving parents, grandparents,
siblings, relatives, and friends of our murdered loved ones.

Ralph L. Myers
November 29, 1994

Prologue

"Looking Back-Looking Forward" recounts my thoughts and ever-changing emotions as we go through the grief process. Each of the six sections represents a different stage of grief and how I viewed or experienced each one. The thoughts and opinions I have expressed are mine and unique to me. Each of us will experience our own personal and private grief after the loss of a loved one.

As a former co-leader of a Los Angeles Chapter of Parents of Murdered Children and other survivors of homicide, I dedicate this book to that organization and feel I owe them a debt of gratitude in helping me get through, not over, the loss of my son Tom... Along this unwanted and unexpected journey, I have met many others who have lost someone to murder, and I thank them for helping me to "get through it" and survive.

Epilogue

Since the murder of my son in 1993, and when I started writing the poems in this book, 32 years have passed. During this passage of time, both of my parents have died, as has my wife's mother, and on September 15, 2015, I lost the love of my life, Francine, when she died due to the complications of pancreatic cancer.

In June of 2012, we travelled back to a California State Prison to attend a parole eligibility hearing for the murder of our son Tom. His mother and I were successful in convincing the Parole Board members not to grant parole to his murderer. In 2018, he was paroled and given a second chance, something my son will never have.

Sadly, after returning from California just two months later, Tom's mother and my loving wife were diagnosed with pancreatic cancer.

Together we have survived the loss of our son, our parents, and now my wife, my soul mate and the love of my life, as I am again Looking Back - Looking Forward at the lives of our son Tom and wife Francine Joan Apostolos Myers.

I dedicate this book of poems to her. She traveled with me and experienced this journey of grief and heartbreak with me, and I don't know if I could have survived without her love, support, and understanding. I love you, Francine.

Your loving husband, Ralph

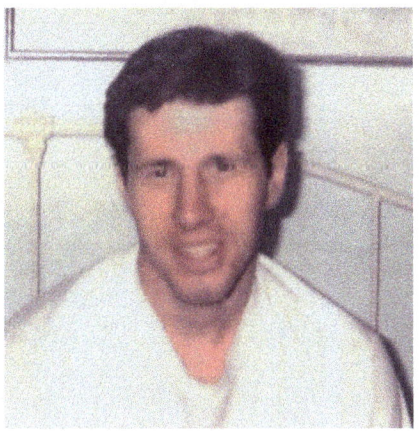

Thomas Arthur Myers

Again, another July 24

Again, the calendar reads
yet another July 24.

Again, loved ones remember and together
they grieve on yet another July 24.

Again, and as always, I think of you my
son Tom, on this yet another July 24.

Again, a year has rapidly, yet it
sometimes feels, gone by agonizingly
slow, on this yet another July 24.

Again, I visit your grave, instead
of the warmth of our loving home
on this yet another July 24.

Again, the pain of remembrance once more
sears our hearts, as we are reminded of the
events that took place twenty-nine years
ago on the night of yet another July 24.

Again, I am there in spirit my son at your
final resting place as I will always be on
future anniversary dates as each one of
them become yet another July 24.

Ralph L. Myers

July 24, 1997

Francine Joan Myers

The Loan

I thank you Lord for seeing fit to
approve my loan; by granting me a
wonderful wife and a son of my own.

The terms and conditions of the
contract are quite clear.

All that is expected of me is a lifetime of
payments due day to day and year to year.

The payments, Lord, I must agree, are
easy to meet because they are free.

Payments of love and affection are to be
remitted daily and year to year, with only the
interest due to tender care and protection.

Though times may be difficult and sometimes
scary, I only have to think of my family and
really, Lord, things aren't nearly as weary.

So, thank you, Lord, for the loan. If I
prove worthy in fulfilling the obligations,
I hope I will be rewarded with an increase
in the loan. I will sit back with fatherly
pride and see how my family has grown.

Amen

This was written and dedicated to my wife,
Francine, on January 24, 1969. I married
her on June 18, 1966, and made the final
payment of the loan, paying it in full on
September 15, 2015, when she died.